A SMALL FAVOR

A SMALL FAVOR
by Anja Meulenbelt

Translated by
Johanna H. Prins
and
Johanna W. Prins

The Crossing Press, Freedom, CA 95019

Copyright © 1980 Anja Meulenbelt
Translation copyright © 1988 by Johanna H. Prins and
    Johanna W. Prins
Cover design by Betsy Bayley
Photo of the author by Camilla van Zuylen
Printed in the U.S.A.

The poetry on the chapter title pages is from a poem by the
Dutch poet M. Vasalis.

Library of Congress Cataloging-in-Publication Data

Meulenbelt, Anja.
    A small favor.

    Translation of: Een kleine moeite.
        1. Meulenbelt, Anja. 2. Feminists--Netherlands--
Biography. 3. Mothers and daughters--Netherlands.
I Title.
HQ1657.M46A3   1989   306.8'743'0924   88-35196
ISBN 0-89594-338-7

I.

Is it today or yesterday, my mother asks,
drifting like a weightless leaf on her white bed.
Always today, I say. She smiles, faintly. . .

1.

About three times a week on my way to work I take line number 10 to the stop at Weteringplantsoen. As I get off I look in the direction of the street where I grew up. The beer brewery is still there, although it does not smell as bad as it did before when the wind came from the wrong direction and my mother had to haul the wet laundry inside because otherwise the sheets would smell of (what was it?) hops or yeast. The playground is still there. The muddy paths through the park, which I was afraid to cross because of the earthworms, are now paved. The large tree is gone. While I was living there it blew over in a storm. But the rest is mostly the same. Along the Weteringschans a Surinam travel agency has gone up. Isn't that where the grocer used to be? The store with the sensible shoes is still there. Also the bookstore where I never see a customer. I bought my first children's paperbacks there. The hairdresser has closed down that horrible place where my mother had my hair cut much too short— even now I feel that chill down my back as the clippers touched my neck. The Boomerang Restaurant still has a sign in its window: "Fresh Mussels Today." I have a photograph of myself at age one-and-a-half or two with bows in my hair walking past that restaurant. The sign said, "Fresh Mussels Today," but in the old-fashioned spelling. We had just moved to Amsterdam.

Three times a week for the last ten or twelve years I have gotten off here, looking in the direction of the street where we used to live. But never in all these years have I walked there to see how the street looks, if the pot-holes for playing marbles are still there, or if it still seems so far to the mailbox at the end of the street. My memories of the place are not happy, unlike Bergen where my grandmother lived. Bergen remains an escape for me even now if I have worked too hard or am lost in too many conflicts. But I avoid this street of my youth, the place where I lived for fifteen years.

I force myself to take a look. Our former house is now an office. As expected, the street is smaller than it seemed back then. Now I am able to see through the windows of the ground floor.

The house is somewhat depressing, makes me want to run away, to indulge myself in new books, new clothes, lunch with a glass of wine.

At first we lived on the second floor. It was an ordinary house, with a living room, bedroom for the parents, a small side room where my brother and I slept in folding beds, jealously guarding our toys from each other. Later when my mother and I quarreled about my rash socialism and her bourgeois ideas, she would recall this period, saying, "We had almost nothing, but I was happier then. Believe me, Dear, money can't make you happy."

The war had just ended. Before we won my father barely finished high school and my mother had graduated from teacher's college but because of the German occupation she never became a teacher. There wasn't much to eat during the war. I was born at the very end of the harsh winter of 1945 and my brother a year later. The doctor said we had a tendency to rickets, "the English disease." Not enough sun, not enough food. Every summer on doctor's orders we went to Pennen on the sea where my parents rented a house. The owners would move to an annex temporarily while we were there. Back then people did not go to the beach as much—only a few families. If you walked five minutes along the beach you would not meet anyone, and you could nestle in the strip of clean white sand between the rows of seagrass and the dunes.

We were not really poor any more, although my mother gave the impression we were. How else could we have rented that house for months and taken our help with us on vacation? And didn't we acquire a car soon after?

During the post-war reconstruction, the trade in office equipment flourished. My grandfather appointed my father to run the business and soon it grew into a family enterprise with a large staff. If my mother ever thought of becoming a teacher, they talked her out of it. The wives of established business owners did not work. She belonged to the post-war generation of women thoroughly indoctrinated with the idea that a good mother ought to be home when her children came home from school.

We became prosperous. I realize this only in retrospect because, like many children from a sheltered background, I assumed it was usual. Everyone I knew was well-dressed, ate Sunday dinners in restaurants where the children were bored to tears, and went abroad for vacation in big automobiles. When the neighbors downstairs moved out we took over their apartments. I got my own room. I didn't know any children outside of the expensive private school which I attended. I did not know the city beyond the bounds of the well-to-do, the Kalverstraat, or rather the P.C. Hooftstraat and the Van Baerle. I cannot remember ever being told so, but in subtle ways it was made clear to me which children I should avoid playing with. The street had a "good" and a "bad" side. Years later it would still frighten me if I ventured beyond the invisible dotted lines, and found myself in the working class neighborhoods where people talked with an accent I had not learned.

We were prosperous but not the kind of people with money rolling out of their pockets, because in a family business extra money is always reinvested. I can still hear my mother say that the housekeeping money was gone and my father's reply "Again?" before pulling the wallet out from his jacket with a sigh. The luxury which I did not recognize as luxury until I married a boy from a lower class was only partially ours. My mother's fur coat and the gold watch, the cars traded in for a newer model at the right time, always the most expensive seats in the cinema, were all these things for our sake, or for the reputation of a successful business man?

Soccer was traded in for the tennis club. Eating hot dogs or french fries was allowed only in places where there was no chance of meeting employees. That was also the reason for keeping the tennis club exclusive, I learned from my father, because tennis partners are on a first-name basis, contrary to the rule that a boss can call his employees by their first names, but the employees may not address him that way. And the first question they asked any young man who came to our house was "What does his father do?"

One of the first articles I wrote anonymously was about my mother. I never told her, not even later when she liked to brag about her daughter the writer, and collected all my books, articles, and interviews. I wrote that first article, "The story of my mother, or, is Mrs. Philips oppressed?" for the women's paper. That was the time of the first feminist groups and our Begatsweh and the leftist boys who thought that only working class women had the right to complain about their lot. Didn't women like my mother have all the privileges of the ruling class with their household help who did all the heavy work? Did they do anything at all, those women with charge accounts at the fancy department store, the women with their second cars and tennis clubs? When I read my story in a circle of other women who brought their stories scribbled in notebooks, I had to stop halfway. To my surprise (did my mother's life affect me that much?) my hands trembled and my voice choked with suppressed tears. "Why don't you read the rest," I said to a woman next me and fighting the emotions that welled up, I listened to the strange voice telling the story of my mother, that life without meaning. The pain of sacrifice, living only for your children, your family, but not really for yourself, until, nearly fifty years old, you were discarded, traded in, put out with the garbage. Of course there was alimony, and in the meantime a move from the street of my youth to an elegant canal house, still with help but without a family making a mess and wanting to be fed. But still, isn't that also oppression? I never let her read it, not only because I wrote of her humiliation in always having to ask for money and our petty complaints about her cooking but also of my hatred. I considered my mother stupid, narrow, and weak. How could she let it happen to her! How could she take it! I never wanted to become like my mother. And in my eagerness to get away I did exactly what so many young women did to escape. Get pregnant. Marry. The same trap she fell into. Why did you let it happen to you, I reproached her. Why did you let it happen to me, I reproach her even more.

"This is her," I say. I show the picture. There she is next to my father. In her fur coat and hat, posed, invulnerable, masked by her lipstick and powder, her eyes hard, her smile forced. "Look," I say, "This was her." The young woman before she was married, both shy and defiant, blond, beautiful, and full of life. Vulnerable. That was her.

If she had not been my mother, would I ever have known her? Would I ever have met her, this lady? Do I know her, have I ever known her?

"Do you remember me?" asks the man behind the bar. I see a man more or less my age, maybe a bit older. "Do you remember where you used to live and the place where you bought your groceries? I was the delivery boy," he says. "I read something about you. Meulenbelt, I wondered, wasn't that the family where I delivered groceries? Ask your mother if she still remembers," he says. "My name is Kees. I always admired your mother, such an elegant woman, so well dressed. You are, how shall I say it, I don't mean it in a bad way, less glamorous than your mother."

My mother. Was she elegant? I don't remember. I think she must have been, with her closets full of clothes and shoes, never leaving the house without lipstick, visiting the hairdresser every week. And yes, when she was the age I am now, forty years old, she was definitely beautiful. But I remember her with a pale face, shuffling through the house day after day in the same gray skirt with the same green sweater until finally the cleaning woman spoke to her: "Why don't you wear something different, you make it look as if *I* am the lady of the house." Elegant?

A girlfriend from long ago confesses later that she had always envied me because of my mother. A normal one. A beautiful one. One who was home when you returned from school. "Jealous of my mother?" I ask in amazement. "I thought your mother was much more exciting—you had art and politics at home." That is what I admired in my grandmother who lived in her own house next to the house of a painter I called Grandpa. Two houses and one garden—an early version of what we now call a live-in relationship. Not as bourgeois as our house.

My mother. It is difficult to fit the images together into one coherent person. The cheerful young mother from my early youth. The cold wife of the company president. The depressed woman, a helpless victim waiting for the divorce that would come sooner or later. At the bank where I go to get money for her with the authorization slip in my hand they ask how she is doing. "Such a lively woman," says the man counting out the money. "It's terrible she's so ill." Lively? My mother? With her eternal complaints? When people from the tennis club stop by, looking too tanned and healthy and physical for the hushed atmosphere of the hospital room, and shake my hand vigorously, I see a completely different woman: my tennis club mother, a cool lady, with a beer in one hand and a cigarette in the other, telling off-color jokes or laughing too loud. Not someone I recognize. And then there is my mother when a man is around, when Ernst comes to visit and her cheeks get flushed; the coquettish gestures from her youth return and not a complaint escapes her lips. "Really she is awful," I tell my lover as we leave the hospital, hurt that she is so nice to him. "She is never that nice when she's alone with me."

I am her oldest child. I should know her better. But do I know who she is? How can I reconcile the courageous, fearless woman who brought Jewish children to safety during the war with the narrow-minded lady of later years. Where is the timid orphan-like girl in the few pictures from her youth, accompanied by a text written by herself in white ink? How do I reconcile the woman who said, "I don't understand what you see in all those women, talk to me," with the Annie from the teacher's college, Annie and her best friend Cathrien lying next to each other beside their bicycles, pages filled with Annie and Cathrien, Cathrien and Annie? The Annie from then and the woman now in the hospital bed, looking confused, eyeing the doctors with suspicion, on the point of dying or not dying.

At her request, after the visit to the hospital I walk to her house to see if everything is still all right and to collect a few items, her checkbook, handkerchiefs. No leaks, no break-ins? I open the front door with the large key. I push, it resists. Her coats are hanging in the hall, one red, one yellow, one green. Her bedroom is exactly as she left it, the bed unmade, telephone on the bedside table, reading glasses, cigarettes, a pile of crossword puzzle books and tennis journals, books by Harold Robbins and comparable Dutch authors. A few of my books are wedged in between. I sit down on the bedspread that was once lustrous and expensive but now is shabbily pinned together on one side with a safety pin. The same twin beds she bought when she got married. It wasn't worth the trouble to have a new bedspread made; the house has been up for sale a long time, with an orange for-sale sign in the window. She wants to leave this place, leave behind the inner city and her fear of squatters and junkies, but most of all she does not want to get ripped off and therefore is asking too much for the house, a price she could have asked last year but not now.

Her bottles of nail polish, hair spray, and perfume stand in a semi-circle on the dresser. Behind that a row of photos of my brothers, myself, the grandchildren, probably the only personal things in this house full of gleaming, impersonal furniture. I let her choose one of the publicity photos taken for my last book because she insisted. As I expected, she chose the most posed shot. "In this one you look friendly at least, not so stern," she says. Next to it in a skewed frame she keeps the sepia picture of her mother, leaning over the swaddled baby that was herself. I found the picture, cracked and stained, during one of my searches into my past, among the disorderly stacks of photos of me and my brother as children, inside a drawer in the room where she keeps her mother's antiques, that is to say, not her own mother, but her father's fourth wife. "Don't you want this enlarged?" I ask. "Shall I have it enlarged for you?"

"Why?" is her response. "I didn't even know her."

"But it's your mother," I say.

"What's the use of delving into the past?" she replies, "all those old things."

But a few weeks later the picture is here on her dresser after all.

The house is hollow, more quiet than ever. The kitchen has not been used for years. The three guest rooms were rarely occupied. I lived in one of them for a year with my little son after my divorce, but that was nearly twenty years ago. The orange cat who usually prowls through the house, plaintively miaowing and looking for company, has been taken elsewhere. "Temporarily," we say, but my mother's return to this house is still in question. None of the faucets drip, there is no dust anywhere. The cleaning woman still comes in three times a week to clean what was already clean.

All sounds come from outside. Cars starting, voices of pedestrians. Standing on the doorstep I enter this time without the familiar ritual: the ringing of the door bell, ding-dong, the light in the stairwell, my mother's footsteps on the stairs, her "yes, yes, I'm coming," the sound of locks and latches, the door pushed open. Her "hello dear," as she turns her cheek toward my kiss, while I brace myself for the first veiled approach. "It's been a long time since I saw you. Wasn't it before Christmas?" No need to turn down the volume of the tennis match on television, her only entertainment in this house much too large for one person, this house she did not want to share with anyone.

In the drawer downstairs, among the photos, is the diary she wrote when she was a student, a notebook with a green marbled cardboard cover. Her fastidious handwriting looks almost the same. Written inside is: "My schooldays at Zetten." She was eighteen. It had not been her decision to go. She was sent by her father who did not want her at home any longer. She was already used to being a stepchild. She never knew her own mother. Her stepmother wanted nothing to do with the little girl. Time after time she has told me what happened when her half-brother was born. His blond curls were allowed to grow, but hers were cut. She was jealous. When she walked her brother in the carriage she would leave it somewhere, run around the block by herself, and hope that someone had taken him away. Each time it did not happen she slapped him before taking him back home. She learned to lie and steal, useful tactics later when she was tired of asking for household money. She would turn my father's pockets inside out before his suits went to the dry cleaner, thought of tricks to get money without his knowledge, and opened an account at the department store that came due in two months so that she would not have to face a small fight every week but only one big fight every other month. The path of least resistance, no direct confrontations for God's sake. She tells me this with some satisfaction but little self-respect.

"I'm good for nothing," she writes again and again in her diary. "If only I could become a good teacher, I'd know what I'm good for. If only Boy (she would eventually marry him) could love me, really love me, I'd know what I'm good for. If only Papa could be satisfied with my grades, I'd know what I'm good for." What does she live for? She has pasted pictures of rosy baby faces in her diary. She wants to become a good mother, a good wife. She wants to have a real family, which she missed--her children will be loved and cared for, they will always have someone who understands them. She longs for Boy when he is not there. When she sees him, she hesitates. Does she feel something, does she love him? Is it really love? Is it really love when she resolves not to dance at her father's party, an anniversary celebration for his business, because Boy won't be there, and then she gives in after all and flirts with Jacques and Wim and Thijs, who keep asking her to dance and want to know if she has ever been kissed. "That evening was not good for me," she writes. "They tell me I am nice, and mischievous, and cute. And admit that you liked it, Annie, but it was not right." Guilt-stricken, she writes

12

to Boy. If only Boy loves her, then she is somebody.

Her father does not approve of her relationship with the young man who has not even finished high school. He forbids her to see him. She gives in and writes him a good-bye letter. Boy despairs, says she should wait for him, and she gives in again. This time it is a secret relationship. Meanwhile her father is divorced and finds a new wife, Kenna. He sends his daughter to a boarding school where she can study to become a teacher. It is nearby and it is cheap. She does not want to go, but she gives in.

She is lonely. She often gets stomach-aches. She hates herself. "I have to learn to give in more often," she writes. The same words I wrote in my diary when I was just married, exactly the age she was then.

At school she lives among women. Boy is almost an abstraction. She writes without emotion about love, in the language of romantic novels, not her own words.

Real excitement and real sadness center around her girl-friends. Nini, Detje, Berta, Dientje, To. They have lovers' quarrels and crushes, although in the innocent 1930s they don't call it that. Cathrien! Of all the girls she likes Cathrien the best. When Cathrien leaves boarding school without saying good-bye, she is broken-hearted, stays in bed with a stomach-ache and writes in her diary: "Why am I so heart-broken? Don't I have Boy?" But Cathrien writes a letter and promises to visit one more time. "Cathrien is coming tomorrow!" she writes. And when Cathrien leaves and she waits for another letter that doesn't come, she is depressed for days. "Really, you are always alone," she writes. "You can't depend on anybody."

She tries to find a new friend. But Nini is already friends with Reina, and they are always together in Reina's room, and even though the doors are not allowed to be locked, when she knocks they won't let her in. At one of their costume parties Reina wears a man's suit and draws a mustache on her face. She and Nini have themselves photographed as an engaged couple. Everyone laughs. She doesn't. When Reina is visiting home, she walks outside with Nini and they share secrets, but when Reina returns Nini will not share Reina and blames Annie for interfering. Nini snitches on her and tells the secrets she just heard, and together they make fun of Annie. "I could have been friends with Nini if Reina weren't here," she writes in her diary. Nini ignores her after that and Cathrien does not write any more. You can't trust women either.

Fortunately there is still Boy, who has asked her if she would like to have his baby. She said yes. Because nothing is more beautiful, more real than motherly love.

I put the diary back with my wedding pictures which she has saved with more care than I have, back with my baby pictures and the pictures of Armin as a baby. When she was not sick, I had no trouble going through these pictures. Now it seems like a rehearsal for the time when she is dead—as if I'm running ahead of myself.

I still have to find her pills. I pull open a couple of drawers in her dresser, slightly nervous, as if I might get caught. More packs of cigarettes. Boxes with jewelry, lots of red and orange, imitation gold and glitter. A gold bracelet that I know she bought after her divorce, as a kind of belated protest against my father who gave her too many household things for her birthdays and too few of the womanly gifts she felt entitled to, like flowers, chocolates, jewelry. Hidden back behind the boxes I see unopened envelopes. They prove to be letters of referral from the family doctor to the specialist. They were never passed on, never read. There are the pills. I try to put everything back in the same place and close the drawers.

Three times I have to pull the front door shut before it locks. On the way down the stairs I nearly stumble.

2.

My mother and I always had a difficult relationship. In an interview with mothers of well-known feminists, she said I was a happy child, a bit stubborn, a bit catty but intelligent. "Until she was about fifteen, I felt I could really talk with her, sitting on the edge of her bed and chatting. I considered her very self-assured: she would make out better in life than I did, I thought." I do not remember one "chat" together, only the fights I always lost. I remember the pillows drenched with tears late at night, the anger I swallowed because otherwise I would have to offer my apologies later on. I remember myself as a misunderstood child and a sullen teenager with brooding thoughts. If anything drove me to feminism it was not the hatred of men that dates from a later time, but the hatred of the kind of woman my mother had become and the firm resolution that I shared with so many early feminists: not to become like her. That first surge in the early seventies was a movement of daughters.

I don't want merely to complain about my mother. She did what she could, what the time told her to do. As children we don't see that our mothers are not omnipotent, that they live within limits not of their choosing, that they have to conform to rules they did not make. I do not like reading books by writers who blame all their neuroses and female hatred on the shortcomings of their mothers. They forgive their fathers who were no better. They are trapped in the child's point of view. Men are in a position to continue blaming their mothers. But I became a mother myself, did everything wrong, had to fulfill an impossible task with contradictory demands. I wanted to do everything better than my mother, to do things differently, but did I really?

Our mothers, our first love, our first disappointment. *Can you talk about your mother without crying?* was the title of an early feminist article. Not me. Nor other women, although at first they thought they could. "Mama has always been an example to me," a woman coolly declares in a group session. Half an hour later she is drowning in tears, stamping her foot with rage as she remembers how humiliated she was by her calm mother who could do everything, who knew everything, who was always right.

"I hate her, that awful woman," I say. "I wish I could still trade her in for a real one." Then I sit there crying like a three-year-old because of all the times I missed her.

My mother remembers the rift between us as the period when I fell in love with a boy. I was fifteen, became pregnant when I was sixteen, and married when I was seventeen. I moved far away with my new family, wrote cheerful, empty letters that hid the fact that I was miserable, that I was a child with a child and a child for a husband. I was in a strange country with strange people from another background. I, the one who was used to central heating, laundry delivered to the door and plenty of money, grappled with a coal furnace and dirty diapers and too little money for the household. When she came one time to see my new place and silently grabbed the Comet to clean the dirty chairs, she must have seen how bad things really were. I was skinny, pale, shy. But she said nothing and did nothing, running away from problems as she had so many times before, and I expected nothing from her any more. For me the rift had happened much earlier.

In one of my subsequent women's groups when we bitched enough about men, we stumbled on a problem that lies deeper in many women and is more painful: our relationship with our mothers. I tried to figure out what happened between us. I definitely knew I felt abandoned by my mother when I was a child. I looked for a trauma but could not find one. She had always been there. Once married, she never made use of her teacher's certificate because of us, she said, my brother and me. She did not punish us much, usually leaving that to my father. She knitted and sewed beautiful clothes, or took me with her to the department store where she picked out brand-new dresses for me. When she went shopping she often brought something back: a necklace, a new sweater. We were overwhelmed with presents on birthdays and St. Nicolas Day. And if she had not always waited for me after school with my homework laid out and my math problems all written up except for the answers, I certainly would have failed a grade once or twice. But all that time I had the strange feeling that it was not meant for me, but for the dream daughter whose part I had to play. She lived through me. She selected my clothes. My large room, decorated in blue and yellow, was furnished by her. If I did not give specific details on my wish list (color, price, store), the gifts I received were what she preferred, not what I wanted. Of course she said I could exchange them, but I knew what would happen if I did that. "Don't you like it? It looks so nice on you. You're not going to exchange it for something trashy, are you? Shall I go with you?" The wounded expression. The explanations. The emotional undercurrent of reproaches about my ingratitude. The beautiful, expensive dolls I received came complete with handmade clothes and fancy names: Claudia, Nicoline, and Joyce. At night in bed I would apologize for all those chic impostors to my ugly first doll, named Jet by me after my favorite grandmother. Even the cat I asked for in order to have at least one warm creature in the house arrived with a readymade name: Cleopatra. Nickname: Patsy.

My mother organized a bridge club for me and my friends when I was in high school. Maybe she wanted to prevent my hanging around in my room with my friends, maybe she wanted to stay in contact with me. "It's so nice to talk with young people," she told everyone. The boys who came loved it. They did not have mothers at home who devoted so much time to them, and they weren't used to being received with bowls full of peanuts and as much cola as they wanted. My boyfriends fell for her. They found her a bit strange, but they kept on coming once a week and sometimes even brought a bouquet of flowers along. For her. I decided I hated bridge and would sulk on the couch or retreat into my room with a book, closing my ears to all the laughter downstairs until I heard them saying goodbye in the hall before my father came home. "Goodbye Mrs. Meulenbelt, thanks very much," they would say, with a yell upstairs: "So long Meul, see you tomorrow at school! I did not go downstairs.

Later, as I am emptying the closets, I find a book that one of the boys gave to her, with the inscription: "For Mrs. Meulenbelt, who was like a mother to me.

3.

Oh God, those Sundays. Sometimes it happened first thing in the morning. Migraine. Pale and suffering, she would stay in bed. The curtains were closed. We had to whisper. "Didn't you notice your migraines always came on *Sunday?*" I ask her later. She looks at me indignantly, as if I am accusing her of faking it. "You can't imagine how terrible it was, Dear. And the doctor couldn't do anything about it, he said it was hereditary and I'd have to learn to live with it."

"Is getting headaches on *Sunday* hereditary?"

She responds with a blank look.

On Sundays everyone was together, and we had to be the happy family my mother had dreamed of in college. For some reason we did not fit the picture.

Other times the tension came later. Sometimes the day began well. I would hear my father whistling in the kitchen, frying eggs. I'd put my book away and climb out of bed. But then, then we would have to do something. We were a family. Families go on Sunday outings. I liked it best when my father took my brother and my mother to the soccer game, so I could stay home, climb back into bed, and read. Once I went along, but my father thought it was a waste of money to buy an expensive ticket for me, when all I did was turn my back to the game and stare at the crowd making fools of themselves. An hour before leaving, the tension would already begin to mount. "Are you coming or not?" my father asked my mother. As usual, she didn't answer with a clear yes or no.

"Then I won't have dinner ready in time. . ."

"Then we'll eat out," my father would say.

"I haven't finished the housework."

"Then leave the beds unmade for once."

"I can't possibly leave such a mess."

"Are you coming or not?" my father would ask, increasingly impatient.

"Why do we always have to go to the soccer game?" she would complain.

"Do you have a better idea?"

"We can do something all of us enjoy."

"Like what?" my father would ask sarcastically.

"You don't have to yell, I've already got a headache."

My father would sigh, look at his watch.

"Whatever you want," he'd say. "If you're ready in an hour, you can come along, otherwise forget it." But after an hour she still would not be ready.

"I'm going," he'd warn.

"I'll be there in a minute," she would yell from the bedroom, or from my room where she was fighting with me because she thought I should be out of bed and dressed before she would leave.

If he waited until she finally came downstairs, they were too late and would fight. If he left by himself, it was too late, and he would be angry and slam the door behind him. Then there would be another fight. But never a yelling match to clear the air. Silence. Suffering. Migraine.

I read a lot in those days.

I hated her for capitulating to my father, for the way she tricked him into giving her money instead of confronting him directly. She tried to teach me to capitulate too: "Be smart, my dear. Men are like children, you have to give them their way." I hated her for her typically female way of fighting back: her depressions and migraines, her suffering. I hated her for the reign of terror at home. *Her* house. Nothing was mine, not my room, not my closet, not my clothes, not the little things I had made. She called it junk. Often when I was in school I would remember with a jolt that I had forgotten to hide something—a doll, a book I had made—and would run home after school to fish it out of the trash in the nick of time.

"Why did you throw that away?" I yelled into the kitchen where she stood cooking inedible food.

"How could I know it isn't junk?" she'd call back.

"You could ask me!" I'd scream.

"I can't wait that long," was her reply. "You'll just have to learn to clean up your own junk."

"But it's *my* room," I'd yell.

"In *my* house," she'd respond.

I always lost. I learned to keep everything that was dear to me far away from her. And not only my belongings, but also my thoughts, my feelings. Maybe that is why I hate her the most: she did not even notice.

Oh, I certainly took my revenge, as only a child, a daughter, can take revenge. Through food. I didn't like anything. The awful soup with the slippery noodles. The putrid endives. My brother didn't eat much either. My father's first question when he came home was: "What's for dinner? That again?" My mother would protest that it was impossible to cook for one person who didn't like this and another person who didn't like that. And when she found something all of us ate without complaining, we would have it time and time again. There was the new artificially pink instant pudding that we ate until we were sick of it and dumped large spoonfuls in each other's bowls when no one was looking. My mother was hurt: "I thought you *liked* this." My father "But not every day, Annie." And she punished us in return. She knew how to ruin even the food we all liked. The steaks turned into tough, tasteless leather, the french fries went limp, the wilted salad with little sour onions that made me gag.

It must have hurt her when I ate dinner with Oma Jet in Bergen, my cheeks red from walking along the dunes. Cucumber salad, homemade applesauce, meatballs and fried potatoes. "Here the girl will gain at least a pound or two," Oma would say with good intentions. I could see my mother cringe.

As a teenager I introduced the first variations on the Dutch menu of meat, vegetables, potatoes. "Fish with cheese?" my father asked skeptically, pricking it with his fork. But because I had made it, and not my mother, he did not push it away. "Delicious," he said. "Did you think of it yourself, or is it a recipe?" I beamed, triumphantly. At least *I* knew how to earn a compliment from him.

II.

She searches—it is an s.o.s.—
for roots and for her youth,
and no one, no one knows her as she was.

1.

"I have to leave," I thought. Leave the house of my parents, where they were unhappy and I was too. I walked straight into a terrible trap just like my mother. But she never talked openly with me about her unhappiness because children shouldn't hear things like that, and so I would rather die than complain to her about the failure of my own life.

When my parents were getting divorced, that is to say when my father wanted to get remarried, I hardly paid attention. I was too preoccupied with my own existence, my chaotic life with a young child and unhappy love affairs. "You should have done it long ago," I said when I heard they were going to separate. I did not think it necessary to take sides. I wished my father a happier life, a partner who didn't complain so much, someone who was interested in his work and enjoyed receiving his friends, someone with a sense of humor and no migraine headaches.

And my mother? She was better off without him, I thought, and she said the same thing. But I failed to see how deeply depressed she was. Wasn't she responsible for having nothing to do, not knowing who she was, what she was capable of, what she was living for? That would never happen to *me*, I thought, as I delved into my studies, politics, the up-and-coming women's movement.

I wanted to have as little to do with her as possible, as if her fate were contagious, as if I would become like her if I got too close.

I did not see my parents often. Every few months on a Sunday afternoon I would visit my father and his new wife, or my mother. The visits were not easy for me. I knew more or less what my parents thought of me: not much. They interpreted my socialism as a rejection of their lifestyle, and they were right. My mother felt that my feminism was a criticism of her life. She was right in that too. I was living in a commune then. Once my mother came to visit, and I can still see how she automatically dusted off the couch before sitting down, refused the cup of tea offered her because she had seen our collection of earless, cracked teacups, none of them matching. With her hands neatly folded over the purse in her lap, knees together, back straight, she sat on the edge of the couch, as if afraid of some contamination in the air, ready to flee.

But she said nothing, fearing another quarrel. Scared, I think that everything she said about my son, who of course walked in wearing the grubbiest clothes he could find, would be interpreted by me as a criticism of his upbringing, scared that I would turn against her with a withering look and a furious sneer about her own child-rearing methods. As if she had been so successful. So a lot remained unsaid.

After that one visit to the commune she did not come any more. Once every few months out of obligation I called her up to arrange a meeting. Sunday afternoon. I smoked too much and drank too much of the sherry she put in front of me. We racked our brains for the next topic of conversation. "Are you still seeing the friend you told me about last time?" she would ask cautiously. "No," I'd say, "that's finished." Silence. I don't tell her that it's finished because he is married. Nor do I tell her that I am now involved with a woman. Later she finds out about it when someone who has read an article in *Sekstant*, says to her: "Isn't that your daughter? She's turned lesbian, hasn't she?" She does not tell me she has heard it, hurt that I did not talk about it and relieved she can pretend she does not know. It's just one more thing. And what will become of my son?

Silence. I stare out of the window. "How is Armin doing at school?" she asks, hoping for a neutral topic. "OK," I answer. "I'll probably fail this year," my son says grinning. She sighs. I can see what she is thinking. "What did I do to deserve this? Where did I go wrong?" But she doesn't say a thing. I don't, either. After an hour or two I am dead tired and want to go home. I have a headache from the continual dialogue inside my head as I sit across from her. She does not seem sorry to see me go. Yet every time I finally manage to pay another visit, she says: "When were you here last, was it three or four months ago?" In reproach.

I wrote *The Shame Is Over* without taking my parents into account. I had not expected that the book would receive so much publicity. Who would be interested in my chaotic life, my adventures in leftist organizations, my series of unhappy love affairs? Surely no more than a small group of big-city radicals and feminists. So I thought. And if my parents did get their hands on it, oh well. They would have to figure out for themselves what to do with it. I was tired of pretending. I would not mind being free of those awkward Sunday visits; clearing the air with a good fight would suit me just fine. They will have to accept me as I am, I thought. Or not.

Since then I have not heard from my father, as if I never existed. My mother reacted differently.

I am always startled when she calls: she does it so rarely, usually waiting for me to call first. When she does call, it means something has happened. She says, "I've read your book." "Oh," I say, feeling my throat close and wanting to slam down the telephone. "Oh."

"Can I stop by to talk about it?"

"Uh, yes," I say. "When?"

"Now," she responds. "I can be there in ten minutes."

"Ok, only I don't have much time, in an hour or so someone is coming over," I lie. Then after I've hung up the phone, sweating, I call a friend to rescue me in an hour's time. "I'm going to have a terrible fight with my mother," I tell him. "She has read my book. She is coming over. Can you come here no later than six thirty?"

She stands on the doorstep, with a bottle of sherry under her arm. I let her in, take her fur coat without looking at her face. I scurry around for sherry glasses. When I finally stand in front of her holding the glasses, she sits down on the couch and to my amazement begins to cry. How long has it been since I saw her crying? Years, years. I stand there feeling awkward. With any other person I would have known what to do, putting my arm around her shoulder, a hand on her knee, offering a handkerchief, but not with my mother. I sit down before her on the floor, shakily fill up the sherry glasses and wait for her to say something.

"My dear," She says, "if only I had known all those things, why didn't you ever tell me? I started reading your book, someone at the tennis club mentioned it, I didn't even know you had written a book, and how could I say that I hadn't read it, that I wasn't even aware of my own daughter writing a book? After the first few pages I threw it into a corner. I thought it was not like that, not like that at all, it could not have been like that. Then I picked it up again and went on reading. Last night at four o'clock I finished. I wanted to call you right away, but I didn't dare."

And then in bits and pieces she begins the story she has never told me. This is the beginning of a series of conversations, attempts to really talk with each other, to clear up years of confusion and misunderstanding.

I was certain that I was an accident. That's how I felt, unwanted. The suspicion was confirmed when a friend of mine who worked temporarily at the city license department retrieved the wedding date of my parents. And yes, my mother was already several months pregnant when they married. I never told them I knew it. They never celebrated their wedding anniversary. I had a plan to bring them a large bouquet of flowers on their twenty-fifth anniversary, but by that time they were finally divorced and it seemed like a sick joke.

"How can you think I did not want you?" my mother weeps on the couch. "I wanted you so much, I was so happy with you, I very definitely wanted you. Everyone said I was crazy to get pregnant while we were still in hiding, unmarried, without food; they said *you're too small, it will be a difficult birth, we have no doctor, you can't even go to the hospital.* But we knew the war would soon be over, and then your father might have to fight in Indonesia. I thought: I will be left behind, alone with nothing, nobody. I didn't care if it was dangerous, and that we would have to move again. I wanted a baby. And now you say it was an accident in your book."

She looks at me, my mother. Her face is blotched. "You have to promise me something," she says. "When you write another book with me in it, will you say that it was not true, that I really did want you?"

I promise.

2.

Of course I must have loved you. You must have been my first great love. I cannot remember the moments when I cuddled against you, when I found you beautiful, when I liked your smell - but these moments must have existed. When I see pictures of myself as a pert little girl with blond curls and apple-red cheeks, I do not feel the heaviness of later years. A happy child. The mother holding me seems nice. How many pictures did you take of me on the beach at Petten with the old-fashioned black camera, stacks and stacks of pictures I keep on finding? Pictures of the little girl I was, naked in the waves, or wearing a knitted bathing suit in colors I still remember: blue with a bit of pink, and I can still feel how scratchy it was when wet. Bows in my hair. A handmade suit with a green jacket and green beret in the park near the Weteringschans or in front of the Boomerange Restaurant. At a birthday party where I wear a party dress with a heart sewn on it in sequins which had taken you hours.

But I learned early on not to trust you. Oh, the dreadful humiliation when you laughed with other people about how you had fooled me. "I'm not making fun of you, it's just that you're so funny," you would say. All those years I had to hear about how you tricked me into eating spinach by giving it another name: hcanips. I am certain I never voluntarily ate the green slop you put in front of me, no matter what you called it, but you were certain you had fooled me.

All those jokes you used to play on me. Later you knew nothing of it. The time you pretended to call the police to get me because I had opened a bag of pepper out of curiosity and spilled it all over the kitchen counter. Laughing, you told other people how I had collected my purse and my doll trying not to cry because I really thought the police were coming for me. I believed you were capable of something like that.

Then there was the time you sent me to the pharmacy for a box of cigars. You meant Tampax, but I did not know about that yet. The pharmacist sent me back. "We don't sell cigars here," he said. "Go ask your mother what she has in mind," but I could tell from the mocking look in his eye that he knew something I didn't know. Howling with laughter, my mother listened to my story when I returned. "Silly girl, I didn't ask for cigars, go back and ask for a box of Tampax." But I had already escaped to my room and refused to participate any longer in adult games I did not understand. I also turned away when she flirted with the shopowners, giggling with the butcher as he prepared sausages for her. I would feel the same embarrassment later when she joked around after drinking one beer too many, she who was so quick to call other people vulgar.

I did not trust you, although I kept trying to win your love. I brought home drawings. "Very nice," you would say. A day later I would find them in the wastebasket. I made clay ashtrays for you, and when I was in high school I made you figurines that would stand on your dresser for a while, only to disappear mysteriously. "My daughter is very artistic," you later announced to other people. But when you were dead I found none of those things. You had thrown away everything.

Almost everything. In a cardboard box I found all the old letters I wrote when I was just married. I did not want to let on how miserable I was and wrote trivial notes full of Armin's newest words, amusing anecdotes about my experiences as a young mother barely nineteen years old in a foreign country. I do not have the letters you wrote back. Were they lost during one of my moves, or did I throw them away?

You taught me to conform. Later you said you admired how as a little girl, I talked back to my father and stood up to him. Precisely what you did not dare to do. But I always had to do it alone. And of course I lost just like you. By the time I was a teenager not much of the headstrong hothead was left. "You did not make it easy for me," my mother says, "you and your brother. You fought tooth and nail. I let you fight, there was nothing I could do. But I saw how it happened. He would tease you and you would tease back - you still have a sharp tongue—until he could not control himself any longer and would hit you. And then you would fight. You were even meaner than he was, you would pull his hair, and once he was totally covered with scratches."

"At school he told everyone it was an accident," she says. "Wasn't that nice of him?"

"I think it was a boy's humiliation after losing a fight with his sister," I respond.

"It was nice of him anyway," my mother insists. "But one time he really did win a fight with you," she adds. "When I came upstairs, he was sitting on top of you. After that you never fought again." I sigh. I have heard the story ten, twenty times. "That was easy," I say, still mad after twenty years. "I was sick!"

"No, not at all," she says.

Are there no happy memories?

We are sitting across from each other at a table in a restaurant nearby in the Leidsestreet, and trying to reconstruct our past together. We are trying to find something, *anything* we both remember, an experience we shared.

"Saturday evenings," you say, "I would give you a bath,

you and your brother, and dry you off on the counter. You looked so pink and smelled like soap, and I would always kiss your bottoms before putting on your pajamas and sitting down the four of us to listen to the radio. *Showboat*, remember? And *The Doorsnee Family*. When we got a television later it wasn't as much fun because we would all sit in silence looking in the same direction."

She looks at me hopefully.

"Yes," I answer, "I remember. And Sunday mornings, we were allowed to get a bowl full of cookies because you did not want to get up yet, and then later the smell of fried eggs with bacon."

"Yes," she says. "Once in a while your father even joined in. We did have some good times as a family, didn't we?"

"Yes," I answer, "we did."

She does not let up. After that first time when she stood at my door with a bottle of sherry and cried on my sofa, she keeps coming back to *The Shame Is Over* again and again. She brings it along with pieces of paper marking the passages she wants to discuss.

"There was something you wrote," she says, "something about how difficult it was to talk to me." She puts on her glasses, leafs through the book, and drops it on the floor. "I can't find it now," she says, "but what did you mean by difficult? I thought we really communicated with each other. I was awake for hours last night. How can that be, I thought, when I considered you such a happy child, and now you write that you were unhappy as if we were always fighting. And somewhere you wrote that I abandoned you. What do you mean I abandoned you? I wanted you so much and I thought: *my* children will have whatever they want. Not like my parents, my mother who died, my father who thought I was too much trouble, my stepmother who really didn't want me. I wanted to spare you all that. Didn't I stay home for you? Wasn't I usually there when you came back from school? You don't mean those few times on Tuesday afternoon when I went downtown, and you were mad because you had to go to the bathroom and had to stand at the front door waiting to be let in, you don't mean that, do you? Those few times?"

She looks straight at me, her gray eyes fixed on mine. Her face is splotchy.

"Why do you say you were unhappy as a child?" She stares at me, holding a fork in mid-air over her plate. She eats almost nothing. Actually we don't come here to eat, only to continue our series of troubled conversations. I prefer to do that in a restaurant where the embarrassing silences are more easily filled, and where it is easier to get up after coffee to bring her home. When we arranged to meet in my house she always stays longer than I can handle. These conversations are exhausting for me. For her too, she tells me later.

I try to think of a good answer. How can I say it without hurting her all over again, without accusing her? "Your dinner is getting cold," I say. "I don't want any more," she says and pushes it away. "You take it." So I finish her plate too. It's poached salmon that I ordered for her because the portion is small. She eats almost nothing. In retrospect, she was probably sick already.

"I remember you clearly as a cheerful child. Very sure of yourself. Decisive. You could handle your father better than I could. Stubborn, you were, really hard-headed sometimes. But if you ask me, you were not unhappy," she insists. "What did I do wrong? Tell me."

But when I begin to tell, hesitating, groping for the right words, how misunderstood I felt, how motherless I felt when she withdrew into one of her depressions, her migraines, her suffering, she interrupts me after a few sentences. She can't bear to hear it. She does not want to hear it. Hasn't she devoted her whole life to motherhood, to her attempts to create a real family? Hasn't she sacrificed everything for that? Didn't she want to give me all those things she had never had? All the clothes. She would regularly knit beautiful sweaters for me. Often she would return from down-

34

town on Tuesday afternoons with new acquisitions and sometimes I had to go along. I was embarrassed by the ritual. "I want this one," I would say when I tried on a dress I really liked, but that was not the end of it by any means. "Have you seen how expensive it is?" she would reply. No, I hadn't. "Don't you like this one better?" No, I did not like that one better. "Don't you even want to try on the other one?" No. Loud conversations with the salesgirl, as if everyone should hear what kind of a daughter she had. "I must look like a fool with such a child. In a couple of months she will outgrow it." Meanwhile I would look in the other direction. "Well all right then," she would say. Then I could take the dress off, and walking to the cash register my mother would add, "Aren't you going to thank me? Aren't you happy with it?" "Thank you, Mother," I'd answer.

How can I explain that I never had the feeling that it was for *me*, but that I had to play a role in her attempt to make us look like a real family? I felt like a dressed-up doll. "My children will have whatever they want." But what did I want? Fewer presents? A mother who did not wait for me to help with my homework when I came from school? Wouldn't I have felt just as abandoned if she had been like the mother of one of my girlfriends, who complained that her mother was never home? Could she have done anything right?

I look at her as she sits there waiting to hear what she did wrong, how she failed in her attempt to make everyone happy and in giving me what she never had. *She* always felt superfluous and with good reason. And should I reproach her for trying to give me what she missed? Hasn't she been through enough already, abandoned in her late forties for a younger and livelier woman? Hasn't she always done what she was supposed to do, giving up her own work after the war for the sake of her husband's career?

Didn't all the experts and popular ladies' journals of that time say that you should give up your work for your children? And what does she have left of the twenty, twenty-five years she devoted to him? An ex-husband she fights with for alimony and the house. Two ungrateful children who come to her grudgingly, obligated to visit her every few months. No, she has not had much in return.

"Mother," I say, "I know you did all you could." She looks at me with suspicion. She does not know if I mean it. And if I do mean it, is that everything? I try to find the words. "I know you did not take a job because of us," I say. "And if you hadn't helped me with my homework I probably would have failed my classes," I add lamely, not very convincingly. I pour her another glass of wine and one for me too. I take one of her expensive cigarettes with the gold-colored tip. "I thought you didn't smoke any more," she says. "I don't," I say, "only once in a while. It's so difficult to explain." "Come now," she says, "you're a writer, you're good at finding the right words. Here it is, *difficult* you wrote. What was so difficult? What have I done wrong? I really want to know this time."

Shall I tell her about the times she locked me into the bathroom, without a light, how I panicked in the dark? I know she doesn't even remember it any more. Shall I talk about her senseless strategies for raising my brother and me with the result that we hated each other? We both earned a dime if he did not wet his bed, so the first thing in the morning I would stand by his bed like a little shrew to inspect him, to see if he was dry. No wonder he hated me. We spent most of our youth fighting like cats and dogs. But wasn't that the way children were raised back then? No, the real problem lies much deeper.

The legacy of our mothers is capitulation. Which feminist wrote that? I resent you most of all because of everything you did for us, negating your own will until all that was left of you was a depressed, suffering, complaining woman. Always giving in to my father. I try to find the words for it.

"You sacrificed yourself, didn't you?"

"Yes," she answers, "around age thirty I gave up my own opinions. If I did have an opinion, we would always fight, your father and I. In my own childhood, I was used to fighting with my stepmother. Sometimes the dishes would fly through the air. And your father also grew up in a fighting household. I gave up my own opinions for the sake of peace and quiet. For your sake. Otherwise it would have been unbearable.

"You know," she says, "I don't know what to call it, but when I was very unhappy a little angel would come and cut the thread and then I would feel nothing. Do you know what I mean?" she asks, looking up at me expectantly, hoping that I will understand, hoping for something we have in common. But no, I don't know that feeling, to the contrary. I would have welcomed a little angel to cut the thread for me once in a while when I was tangled up in too many strong emotions. Other people would turn to drink, or drugs, or a little angel. But no matter what I did, the pain got worse. "It's a flaw in my constitution," I said in my discussion group, "No thermostat. I never cool off." But cooling off was easy for my mother, I understood later. When she could not handle things any more, she simply pressed the button. And often she was not able to handle things. Other people remember her as a vital person, a charming woman. I remember her as gloomy and absent-minded. She swallowed pain killers as soon as she sensed anther migraine coming on, and at times that was almost daily. I can still see the drawer with the bottles of Optalidon she hoarded, afraid it would no longer be available since it was being withdrawn from the stores. Were you already destroying your intestines and stomach with those drugs?

    You were not happy, I saw that. But you were determined not to show it, not to make us suffer with you. From the time I was very small I can remember the fights, the yelling in the bedroom, the crying afterward with me shyly standing by. Then it seemed as if you still had emotions, that you were still alive. But later, no. Later you walked like a zombie through the house in your gray skirt and green sweater and compulsively ran the household. Monday the bathroom and the stairs. Tuesday the children's rooms. Wednesday the dining room and the kitchen. Like a robot. Cursing the mess everyone left behind. Cooking mechanically, without love, a dinner that no one ate with any gratitude. The cupboards were full of cleaning powders, furniture wax, and bleach, as if the war was still on and you had to keep extra provisions. "You were always polishing," I tell her later. "Sometimes I felt like an oil stain, or garbage, as if I could only be in the way, a burden to you."

    She looks at me, astonished.

    "I *hated* housework," she says. "I did it for you. I hated it so much that the only way I could manage was to hold myself to an exact schedule. And all that fuss about dinner. From the day I got divorced I've never cooked again. Never again."

    "I saw that you weren't happy," I say to her. "Can you imagine it is hard for children to have a mother who is always unhappy?" She looks at me. "I did my best not to show you," she says, "not to cry when you were around. I remember one time I was fighting with your father, we fought a lot at first. He slapped me and I fell. You were dancing on the sofa and I stood up and danced with you, as if it had been a game. Can you remember that?"

I shake my head.

"Why didn't you divorce earlier?" I ask her. "Didn't you ever think about it?"

"Once I was on the point of leaving," she answers. "A good girlfriend told me to take my daughter and go. I was in love," she says, blushing, "a very charming man, I could really laugh with him. He wanted me very much, child and all. But then it turned out I was pregnant again. And my girlfriend left town. I never saw her again. I did not have the courage, I felt it wasn't right. Not after all the divorces I had gone through. Your father's parents were divorced, my father was divorced. I thought it was terrible for the children. I didn't want to do that to you. So I decided to stick with it."

"And then the little angel came to cut the thread," I say. "Yes," she replies, "that's how it was. Then I didn't feel anything any more."

I fall silent, looking at her across the table, this lady who is my mother. I still find it difficult to bridge the gap. I put my hand on hers.

"I think I've done everything wrong," she whispers.

"No," I say, "no, aren't things better now?"

"Yes?" she wonders. "Is that true?"

"We can talk with each other again," I say.

She nods, blows her nose.

"May we have the check, please," she asks in her lady's voice. She allows herself to be helped into her fur coat. "Nice waiters," she says as we walk outside. "I especially selected them for you," I say. "I thought you would like those nice young men."

I link my arm in hers to walk her home. "You can tell they're gay though," she says.

"Oh, Mother."

At her door she says, "Don't wait too long before calling again. Otherwise I'll start thinking that it isn't really true that we are friends now."

"I won't wait too long," I respond, "but you can always call me, too." "That's still difficult for me," she says.

When I got pregnant, my mother knew before I did. I suspected nothing. "You were in love," my mother says, still with a tender look in her eyes. Was I? After the misery of that marriage, can I still remember being in love? I must have been. It was a romantic vacation. The Austrian lakes, my first wine with dinner, I was fifteen. The ugly girl with the gangly legs and the ragged hair had grown into a teenager who in the picture had all the charms of a fifteen-year-old: a blond ponytail, a waist that could be circled with two large hands, and young breasts. I enjoyed the attention I received. I was excited that the boys looked at me when I waded into the water in my bikini. But perhaps my mother found it even more exciting than I did.

At any rate she was the one who urged me to introduce the young man who was most insistent in his attempts to swim after me and corner me in the reeds. And she was the one who suggested I ask him to visit us for a week in Amsterdam, after we had sustained an awkward exchange of letters for several months. I remember he was disappointing, the young man who had made an impression on me in Austria with his strong shoulders who now seemed smaller than in my daydreams, not so well dressed in trousers slightly too short, and clumsier. It was easy to be in love with him from a distance, waiting for his letters full of cliches, but now that he stood in front of me I really did not know what to do with him. Was I still in love? My mother thought I was. "You became sexy at such a young age," she says, "you had bedroom eyes." Me? I was still trying to defend myself against the boy's pushy sexuality; I certainly did not feel sexy. Yes, I did feel desirable, and I enjoyed it. I felt grown-up, adult, and proud to be the first in my class who had a real sexual relationship.

My mother did not stand in the way of his advances. To the contrary. Before he came to Amsterdam for a second time she tried to give me a mini-lecture about birth control, about safe and unsafe days. "Mother," I cried out irritably, "I haven't gotten that far!" But you said, "You never know." And when my lover was visiting again she would send him to my room in the morning to wake me. Never said a thing when it took hours before we came downstairs, with him snickering and me humiliated. Knew immediately that "it" had happened and asked with tears in her eyes if he really loved me. Restrained my father who suspected that the house guest was not sleeping in his own room at night but sneaking across the hall toward my bed where I lay in the baby-doll nightgown my mother had bought for me.

A few months later I felt nausea in the morning. The next day again. Innocently I thought I had the flu. My mother took me to the family doctor, an old-fashioned patriarch, who announced to my mother that I was pregnant. While I slowly realized what that meant, my mother was already organizing everything. I remember I wanted an abortion and that my mother made one attempt to ask a nurse friend of hers about the possibilities. She came home with the news that it was not possible, that the doctor in question did not do it any more. Years later she does not remember ever discussing an abortion. "You were so in love," she says again, "and you wanted the child so much."

She went to the school to discuss my condition. The principal said I would have to leave, I was a bad example for the other girls. My mother found a gynecologist for me and organized prenatal classes. She wrote a letter to the boy demanding that he marry me and contacted his parents. She arranged the wedding, a discreet small affair and took me, arm in arm, to the P.C. Hooft shopping district to buy a three-piece suit and black shiny pumps. All I had to do was say yes. In her house, where I would continue to live until my husband-to-be had found a job and I could join him with the child, the layette began to accumulate. Diapers in fashionable pastel colors, navel bandages, "What are those, Mom?" I asked. Rattles, teething rings, baby bottles, a cradle, a baby carriage, baby soap, baby oil, talcum powder, I stared at the piles of things, agreed that the side room should be painted in pastels, and tried to understand that this was real. Fuzzyheaded, as if under the influence of drugs, I sat in a chair with my huge belly and tried to make a few bibs, tried to feel the way I thought an expectant mother should feel. But needlework has never been my strong point, and my ragged garments made a poor showing next to the stacks of cottony-smelling baby clothes that my mother had already purchased. I never finished them.

They practically had to force my mother out of the delivery room; she wanted to be there. When I came home from the hospital she was always busy with the baby, told me what the feeding times were, put his diapers on, had herself photographed with the baby on her arm. One time I awoke from my daze and fought with her. I can't remember why, but I do remember leaning over the staircase of my attic apartment, yelling at my mother downstairs: "It's my baby, my baby, not yours."

My mother, deeply wounded, did not speak to me for days until I apologized. How could I have said such a thing after all she had done for me?

Now, after several conversations, I begin to understand what happened back then. I see how much she was trying to relive her own past through me. She herself had fought like a lioness for a baby against everyone's advice, against my father's hesitations about having a child at that time while she was still in hiding during the war. She had hoarded bottles of tomato juice to feed me and packages of powdered milk. She was convinced that I wanted my baby as much as she had wanted hers and that no one should try to stop it, neither the prospective father, nor his parents who wondered if their son was too young to get married, nor my father who had observed all this with embarrassment and disapproval. No one. And it would not be as difficult for me as it had been for her; my child would have everything.

She lived through me, I realize now. She projected her dreams onto me, tried to fulfill her old desires through me. Later she confessed a little mischievously that she had gone on a vacation by herself after the divorce to the same lake where we had been earlier as a family. For a while she had had a lover with the same first name as my young husband and the same nationality. And almost the same age. "Isn't that a coincidence," she says to me with twinkling eyes and then more sadly, "I had to end it. It was impossible at my age. I couldn't, with such a young boy.

3.

In the most difficult time of our lives we couldn't help each other. "I never told you how lonely I was," she says. "I never told you either," I say. I never told you how unhappy I was in my marriage, with my young husband whose parents had taught him only one response to any situation that got out of hand, violence. He had just come of age and was absolutely unprepared for the life of a responsible husband supporting a wife and child. We were stranded somewhere in France where he thought he could earn money by betting on horses. I was sick, our savings were gone. We decided to go back to Holland to look for a place to live and another source of income. My parents agreed to let us move into their empty guest rooms until he could find work and a house. But the welcome was not whole-hearted. My husband had no intention of getting a real job or starting some sort of study; after lying in bed all day, he disappeared in the evening for mysterious appointments. I was sure he was going to a cafe where he could bet on horses and have contact with marginal underworld figures; my parents only suspected it. Of course I felt their disapproval and withdrew to the room with my son who had just turned two, away from my meddling parents and their well-intentioned but impractical advice. Finally, a straw broke the camel's back. We had gone to a film, my teenage husband and I. Armin was sleeping when we left. I placed his potty in the corner of his bed in case he woke up. He had just learned what to do with a potty. Apparently he did wake up and sat on it. And when my parents came upstairs to see if he was all right, they found the entire bed and himself smeared with poop. There was no discussion, only some incoherent yelling up and down the stairs, *antisocial good-for-nothing*, and the next morning my mother came with my father's ultimatum. The boy had to have a job within a week, otherwise we would have to leave.

We left for an illegal room in an alley in the Jordaan district of Amsterdam where I would experience the darkest period of my life, depressed to the point of suicide, introversion, agoraphobia, nightmares. In my memory the months blend into one single image: the rain pelting against the blind wall we saw through our only window and the smell of the smoking petroleum stove.

"I knew that things were not going well with you," says my mother. "I saw you were trying to hide it. Yes," she says and even laughs a bit, "you did not learn that from a stranger, did you? I always hid from you how awful I felt. But I did not realize how awful it was until I read your book. If you only knew how I blame myself for not helping you. I didn't even know where you lived, but on the street I always looked around for you."

She begins to cry.

"I should not have let you go. But your father did not want you any more, and I could not go against him."

"And then a little angel came and cut the thread, so you felt nothing any more," I say.

"Yes," she admits, "that's how it was. When you can't do anything about it, it's better not to feel anything at all, don't you think?'

"But I did not have much help from *you* when I was going through hard times," she adds.

I nod.

"Did it ever occur to you to ask me how I was doing right after the divorce?" she asks.

"No," I say, "I never thought of it. You would never have asked me for help, never."

When I was finally divorced I moved back in with my

parents for a few months in their new house along the canal, in the attic together with Armin. Every day I was afraid, especially when my ex threatened to kill me or take his son out of the country where I would not be able to find him. But every day I dared to do a little bit more, to walk further down the street, talk to people I did not know, contact the people I used to know. An old friend who had been in love with me at school came by. A shy boy, the opposite of Armin's father. Under the anxious scrutiny of my parents and his we began a relationship. His parents were against it: why should their son have anything to do with a girl who already had a child and a divorce before she was twenty-one? My parents were also against it. We clung to each other as if we were drowning, he and I. He stopped drinking and took Armin to kindergarten on his bicycle. I learned that making love could be fun once I helped him over his shyness and we began to explore our bodies together, cautiously, as if we were discovering everything for the first time.

"Do you remember when Jonas came by and we slowly began a new relationship?'

"Yes," she says. "I was so afraid you would make another mistake. That boy hadn't even finished school, and he was already drinking. I thought, oh God, not another drama, I wanted you to be happy, and Jonas was. . .weak.

"Jonas was a sweetheart," I reply, "very gentle. I learned how to make love with him. And he was crazy about Armin."

"But later things did go wrong," she says defensively. "I could see that things weren't going well, he couldn't stand up to you. I wanted to protect you from another disappointment."

"I noticed that," I say. "Remember what you did, one time when he came to my room up in your house, and we had put Armin in bed and were just starting to make love very cautiously because he was shy and I was still a little afraid of it, and you came upstairs and called *It's midnight, that boy must go home, this isn't a flophouse.*"

"No," says my mother, shocked, "no, that can't be true, I didn't say that. Is it really true?"

I laugh. "Yes, yes," I say, "an unforgettable sentence. I couldn't have made it up."

"Do you think that we can still work things out?" my mother asks. "But things *are* better now," I assure her. "You are doing much better now that you are living alone. And I'm doing better too. And we talk, we talk more than we have in all our life together."

"Well, give me your arm then," she says, "but don't walk so fast. You're just like your father."

"At the tennis club someone said as a joke: is that feminist your daughter?"

Her eyes are gleaming.

"When I said yes he didn't believe me at first. Well, he said, who would have thought it, she certainly doesn't get it from you. Then I said: "You'd better be careful, young man, you don't have any idea how much of a feminist I am." She laughs with me in a conspiratorial way.

She used to be afraid of my feminism and complained that I was turning into another one of those bitter, sour, man-hating types. Of course she also had the feeling it was her fault. If only she had prevented that awful marriage of mine, if only my second lover had been a real man, not a weakling.... Naturally, after all those bad experiences, I would turn to a relationship with a woman. At least my lover was not so bad. Very...nice. Very normal, really. Also a woman with children. Maybe, she reasons, it is understandable that women who have had a rough time with men seek each other out. Many years later when I take up with a man again, she is almost disappointed. She had just gotten used to the idea, even enjoyed telling people in an offhand way when they were making jokes about lesbians, "My daughter is one too. Got something against it?"

I seem to be doing pretty well for myself.

Armin is normal; he is going to school and he is not on drugs. And when she sees how close we are, mother and son, it hurts her that I could not have been like that with her, friends sharing private jokes.

She even seems to be proud of me.

Once she walked into the bookstore where she usually buys her books, saw that my book was pushed to the back, and when no one was looking moved the stacks around so that my book would be up front again. She is also proud that the book was reviewed on television. I was pleased about it too but for another reason. A working class woman had described how much it meant to her, and I felt honored and validated because I had managed to write a book that was read even by people who otherwise did not care much for books.

"Couldn't they have done it . . ." My mother gropes for the right word, because she has already seen that she made me mad. "Couldn't they have done it on a slightly higher *level?*" she asks.

"What do you mean *level?*" I ask. "Well," she says, "by not using someone with a *vulgar* accent, as if they did not want to pay extra for someone who speaks proper Dutch. Surely everyone can speak proper Dutch if they try?" she asks defensively watching my face.

But now she looks for the things we have in common. She needs trust, the bond she thought we had when I was young but which I tell her now existed only in her imagination. She is warming up to feminism. Her version of feminism, that is. It begins when I ask her to talk more about her marriage, not because I really want to hear it, but because I see how much effort it takes her to keep all the suffering inside, how often she sits with her lips pursed and hands clasped over her stomach. Her stomach hurts. She felt humiliated when after some twenty years of marriage he took off with a younger woman, but she swallowed the bitterness, denied her loneliness. Her cleaning woman knew how depressed she was. "I am going to jump into the canal," she once said. "But Ma'am, you know how to swim," answered the cleaning woman in an attempt to make a joke out of it.

"I always thought you would side with your father," she says. "You take after your father, you're just as stubborn, just as critical. . ." But then the torrent breaks loose, all the great and small humiliations, the bitter fight over the house where she still lives, the staking out of territory. "He won't chase me out of the tennis club. Let him go somewhere else, with his. . ."

It seems to relieve her. She takes another beer and, slightly tipsy, the flushed cheeks, tells me everything, beginning with her father and then her husband. An insect scurries across the floor to the bench where she is sitting. "Men," she sneers, "men!" and crushes the bug with her beer can. I feel slightly sick to my stomach.

Men is the theme around which much of her life turns now. Her fight against men. All attempts to fend for herself as a single woman fall into that category. The whole world is against her, and the whole world consists of men. The plumber, the people at the bank, the real estate agent, the tram conductors, the parking lot attendants, the doctors, the window washer, the squatters, the mayor: men. "If I get on the bus and the conductor pulls up before I can punch my ticket, then I simply don't pay," she declares with satisfaction. "They see you getting in, and then they start driving before you've found a seat just for the heck of it." She shows me one of the letters she is writing to the city in her eternal struggle against the men who are tearing up the street in front of her house and restoring the bridge. "Working, ha!" she says. "All they do is drink coffee, making it impossible for me to park the car at my front door. But I have written a letter about this," she says. After she dies I will find a stack of neat letters in her neat teacher's cursive writing, with "Dear Sirs" at the top and then her grievances, point by point. "Yesterday I hit my limit," she says. "For weeks now they have blocked off traffic in front of my house. When I return from the tennis club I can't find another parking place, and after all I live here. So I got out, pushed the barricade to the side, and parked the car in my usual spot. This morning as I am leaving the house to get the car, one of those guys comes up to me and says, Your car should not be here, Ma'am, and I say to him, 'Young man...' Now her voice is cutting, full of snobbish sarcasm: "'Young man, I happen to live here, and surely it is clear that I cannot find place for my car anywhere else.'" That led to a quarrel which ended with the man, blind with rage, hurling the fence into her car and breaking the sideview mirror. But my mother always has the last word. She managed to say to him as he was walking away, "Am I dealing with a gentleman or a boor?!"

And then there are the squatters. Driving home from the tennis club, she was held up by a demonstration. She had drunk a few beers and needed to go to the bathroom urgently. "I couldn't do it in my pants, of course, nor in one of those porticos where the common boys do it. So I thought, I will carefully push onward, they should be able to let me through. Then those boys began to hammer with their fists on the roof of my car. You know what they said?" She shudders visibly and whispers: "Cunt. That's what they said. To me!"
Men.

When her old black tomcat died she wanted a new one. "Why don't you get a female?" I said. "They're much easier to keep inside." But no, she wanted a male and got one, a feisty red fireball who grew into a muscled, lion-like beast within a few months. From the very beginning it was war. The cat was bored stiff so he climbed the curtains, forced open the cabinets, pulled groceries out of the bag with his sharp fangs and scattered the contents over the floor. But most of all he enjoyed playing with my mother, landing under her sheets with a flying leap just as she was getting into bed or jumping on her neck when she sat down. Finally my mother started keeping a rolled-up newspaper to rap him if he did something he shouldn't. WHAP! Whereupon the cat gleefully threw himself into the fray and attacked her ankles every time she descended the open spiral staircase carrying a tea-pot. Whereupon she grabbed the newspaper downstairs, WHAP WHAP. "A tough guy," she yelled at me. "Do you see? A real tough guy. Always wants to be boss." And WHAP she would go again with grim satisfaction.

Men.

"Don't you think so?" she says.

"Uhh. . .yes," I say.

We see each other once every two months. I don't live far from her and now that our relationship is not so strained any more I try to come more often, for a shorter time. But my attempts to drop in now and then for a cup of coffee or a drink after work don't work out. When I walk past her house and see the light on I ring the doorbell: "I'd like to drop in for a minute, if you're not busy."

"For a minute?" she says, raising one eyebrow. She needs more time than that--she hasn't seen me in weeks and in the meantime she has thought of questions, topics she wants to discuss with me. When I set down in her orange chair she takes a while before coming to the point.

"I had so much to talk about," she says. "I even wrote it down, but when you're here I suddenly forget."

"We have time," I say.

51

"Don't you have to go somewhere tonight?" she asks. "I know you're busy."

"No, I don't have to go anywhere," I answer.

She relaxes a little.

It still bothers me you wrote about how difficult it is to talk with me," she says. "We have a lot of things in common, don't we? No?" She looks at me searchingly.

"But we also have differences," I say.

Why can't I simply stick to the things we do have in common? I still have the need to be seen as a separate person, not as her extension. Too much of my life she thought she knew what was good for me, what went on inside of me. Even now, nearly forty years old, I am trying to detach myself from her, trying to earn approval for choices that are different from hers. And each time she is deeply hurt when I emphasize my own point of view, my own vision. About class, for example.

She never uses the word which comes from my vocabulary, not hers. But even if my socialism is not as dogmatic as it was ten years ago, when I wanted nothing more to do with my entrepreneurial family, I still can't accept the unquestioning belief that each person creates his or her own fate.

"Your father began as bicycle repairman, after all," my mother says. "When he was building up the business it was not beneath him to transport the adding machines on a three-wheeler."

"But would he have come that far if he hadn't had your father's financial support?" I ask.

"Anyone can be successful if he works hard enough," she responds.

I used to revel in poverty, the way rich kids rebel against their parents. I had an apartment in the working class district of Amsterdam and as a matter of principle sent my son to a public school, not one of those elite private schools where my parents had sent me. "My dear, how your language is changing," my mother said to me when I came to dinner after working with a group of young blue-collar workers, telephone company apprentices, boys who had left school at age fifteen. In my well-meant solidarity with the oppressed classes I began to speak their jargon to provoke my mother. I didn't believe that the working classes would rise and seize power from property owners like my parents. Once in a while I even felt some respect for free enterprise; didn't I enjoy negotiating contracts with publishers and participating in the establishment of a new company? "You've got more of your father in you than you're willing to admit," Ernst observed, "your nose for business, your efficiency in starting a new project." I admit with some reluctance it is true. And, looking back, I also see how much work it was to keep a business going, much more work than the stereotype of a fat capitalist getting rich sleeping while his subordinates work themselves to the bone, which is what I had been taught in my various workgroups.

But it still bothers me, the narrow-minded outlook of the middle class, the automatic, polite condescension toward people without money, the tendency to treat people who do not come from the same background as servants.

"What do you mean?" my mother wants to know when I made a sarcastic comment about the tennis club. "Doesn't everybody go to the tennis club? Doctors, but also the police, business people. . ."

"The unemployed," I ask, "welfare mothers?"

"Well, no," my mother hesitates, "but if they wanted to they could join as well."

An then there is her house, the five story mansion she inhabits alone. But does she use that house? She uses the easy chair in front of the television and her bed. She uses the spacious kitchen only to fry an egg once in a while and to make tea. The dining room is never used. When I ask her one time if a friend of mine who left her husband could use her guest room for a couple of weeks, she refuses. She doesn't want strangers in the house. I don't say anything. I don't say "How can you leave half a house empty when there is a housing shortage, how can you refuse one of your guest rooms to a woman who has nowhere to go?" She knows me well enough to read the disapproval in my face and starts to defend herself. I know the cliches. Money can't make you happy. That is true. I can see it. She has money and she is unhappy. "Nonsense," she replies when I point out that it is still better to be unhappy with money than without. "In the war I lived in a single room with nothing, no food, and your father painted plywood dolls to earn a little money. And after the war we had nothing, don't you remember how it was without a bathroom when I bathed you on Saturdays in the wash-basin? No laundromat, the wash on a rack near the stove, remember? And was I unhappy at that time? Did I complain I did not have enough money?"

"You had a way out," I say. "Everyone has a way out if they want it," she replies. "You began to study when you were divorced and had a small child. You can do anything you want," says my mother who never studied after teacher's college and never earned her own keep.

"How would you have liked standing in a welfare line holding out your hand?" I argue.

"Well," she answers, "I would have found a solution, I would have found work, I have my teacher's certificate and there are other kinds of jobs I would have liked, something in a hotel, hostess, receptionist, something like that. . ."

I fall silent. I am ashamed of my own nastiness, criticizing her like this. She is no opponent. And what do I gain from making her realize that she would be nothing without her money? Doesn't she feel enough of a failure already?

In the years that follow my old resentments gradually

54

dissolve. I recognize my own narrow-mindedness, my easy condemnation of her life. I see that the house is the only thing she has left and that is why she defends it with all her might. It gives her security, the status she cannot get any other way. I feel a new and growing respect for her when she tells me she has created a special role for herself at the tennis club as coach for the children who play tennis there, helping to organize tournaments, keeping contact with the parents. "My work," she says, although she is not paid for it. "She is a pretty courageous woman," I say to Ernst, slightly surprised at this insight. "She was really quite plucky after the divorce, not letting them chase her out of the tennis club and really making something of her life. And without any support. She certainly had no support from me, she did it all alone."

"You two are more like each other than you are willing to admit," Ernst says.

"Oh, spare me," I respond. "After years of trying so hard not to be like her, is that the result?"

But perhaps it is true.

But, still, things are not easy. I smoke and drink too much when I have a date with her, return home exhausted by the difficult groping for words, the attempts to be honest without wounding her again, the struggling not to fall back into my childhood patterns, not to rebel against her when she irritates me. But we have gained something.

4.

I remember her saying: "I was happiest during the war." She would say it during our fights. I never asked her why or how.

A year or two before she became ill, I was participating in a group with a few other women to discuss the differences between women. The majority of the group was Jewish, the minority, myself included, non-Jewish, but each in her own way was interested in the question of Judaism. Personal experiences during the war, parents in the resistance, or, more difficult still, parents who had collaborated. One of the women lived in Germany as a girl and saw fourteen and fifteen year old boys shot as deserters. Another woman realized in the course of the group discussion that her grandmother had been Jewish. That meant her mother was Jewish too. And she herself. "Well I guess I'll be going," she said when it dawned on her she had joined the wrong half of the group. She is confused. "I didn't think it would matter so much," she says. "At home we never observed any Jewish traditions, my mother never talked about it. Strange, isn't it, that it does matter, so much so that I now feel I can finally go home." I don't find it strange at all, because I have seen how each of us carries our family history and how we try to deny precisely those things that cannot be repressed. I am the child of my parents, the daughter of my mother, like it or not.

"Do you have to know?" my mother asks when I come to her for the history of my family during the war. "All those old stories, do you really want to hear them?" I try to explain why. I have noticed that almost all of my real loves were Jewish and many of my friends as well, as if I seek them out. "There are not that many left here," I say. "It can't be coincidence." Then I ask: "Why have so many members of our family, as far as I know, married or remarried someone

Jewish? Isn't that aunt Jewish?" I ask, "and the son-in-law of Grandma's friend, and how did Grandma get her Jewish name?"

"I really don't know," my mother replies. "I never stopped to think about it. It makes no difference to me, Jews or non-Jews, we're all human beings."

"And what about the dreams I had as a child," I tell her. "All those nightmares about men coming to get you. The boots on the stairway. Uniforms. And something else -- when I was small you once took me to a family who lived behind a shoe store. It was dark and mysterious and it smelled like leather, what were they doing there?" "My God, Child, do you remember that?" my mother says. "That was the family P., they were also in hiding. You must have been very young."

"Why were we in hiding?" I ask. "I just read an article in the newspaper about an underground movement that brought Jewish children to safety. The name Meulenbelt was mentioned. Did you participate in that?"

"You know that," she says. "I've told you before, but you never wanted to listen. And, well, what I did was not so important really. At the end of the war suddenly everyone seemed to belong to the resistance. So they say. The people who really did something preferred to keep their mouths shut. You can't go around advertising yourself. You simply did it, you couldn't just let those people suffer, you couldn't just let them be deported. That's nothing to boast of. Really, we should be ashamed that we didn't do more, that there weren't more people helping out.

Her father, for example, that coward.

And now the stories come out. In bits and pieces, all at once. She does not remember much. She's not sure how she got to be a messenger. "I think your uncle asked me or your grandmother. They needed women. They attracted less attention walking along the street or sitting in the train with a group of children. They needed many women, because the same faces passing by with different children would cause suspicion, and then the children and the entire organization would be in danger."

"My father never lifted a finger," she says, "and that's why I did not want his name back when we were divorced. Once I brought a child to a new address and the people suddenly lost their nerve which happened quite often. So all of a sudden there I stood with a child on the street, and I couldn't bring him back. I wanted to bring him to my father who lived nearby with his new wife. I did not let them send me away, but how nervous they were! The child did not know what to do, he was stir-crazy from being inside for so long. And my father was afraid of the noise because of the neighbors. The next day I had to take the child away, otherwise they would leave him out on the street or something. Of course I brought him to another address the next day. But imagine, a few weeks later my father came crying to me, asking if I would help some Jewish friends of his find a new address. The hypocrite.

"When I was pregnant with you, he wanted nothing to do with me. When is that supposed to happen, he would ask, pointing at my belly. And I remember he opened a cupboard to show me the things he had hoarded. Rows of peas in glass jars, with a layer of fat on top. Whole hams. My mouth watered. I was pregnant and had practically nothing to eat. He gave me nothing, not a thing."

"Weren't you afraid?" I ask.

"Afraid? Never," she replies. "Maybe I was too young to know the danger," she says. "Sometimes we were reckless. For a while your father was in hiding at a farm and came back to Utrecht with a beautiful brown tan. In the city everyone was white and skinny. You might as well have stamped 'Person in Hiding' on his forehead. No," she says, "I was never afraid. It was better to do something than just sit at home waiting. It was awful to think that the Germans might come when there were ten Jewish children up in the attic, or later when your father and uncle were also hiding up there. But if I had something to do I wasn't afraid.

"Back then I worked for the Dutch Railways. But at a certain point I couldn't do that and the resistance work. I still regret leaving my job without explaining why. I lived in a room close to the house where the children were, a temporary address. Once I was there during a search. I had left the food coupons for the children in my bicycle bag downstairs. They forgot to search it. Who are you? they asked me. I stood there, pretending to be very small and shy, and said: 'I am a friend of Mrs. Meulenbelt.' They were already looking for me. I was too well-known in Utrecht. If they had found the coupons they would have captured the blond bitch, as they called me. Then you wouldn't have been born.

"Sometimes it was very difficult. You had to take children away from their parents in order to bring them to safety. Sometimes the children did not want to go. You had to keep them quiet with a white lie. I remember standing at a new address with a child on my arm who began to cry, *This is not where Aunt Judy lives, this is not where she lives.* You had to be tough sometimes. Once I retrieved a child from an address we did not trust any more. A boy in uniform and I wearing a Dutch National Socialist pin took the child away. You should have seen those people stare at us!

"No," she admits, "I was not so courageous. There were women who dared to take three or four children at the same time. One of them dressed up a whole group as a birthday party with party hats and funny noses and brought them away like that. And you always wondered how Jewish they would look. I remember a boy who looked so Jewish, he might as well be wearing a yarmulke. And what a chatterbox he was! I was sitting with him on the train and could see the people across from me wondering what a blond woman was doing with such a dark boy. And he kept calling out: 'When are the German police coming, Aunt Annie, when are they coming?' A woman sitting across from me saved the situation by saying: 'What a cute little Indonesian boy you have.'"

"Ah, and then there was little Max," she says. "I had to pick Max up from people who were not allowed to know I came from an underground organization, they were not allowed to know who I was. But Max knew me because I had already picked him up several times. I could only hope that he would keep his mouth shut until we were outside. Some children sensed exactly how they should act. When we got outside he finally said to me, 'Aunt Annie, where are we going now?' I saw Max a couple years ago in a department store. No, I did not talk to him. I thought he might not want to be reminded of that time. It is so painful for many people. No," she continues, "I never heard from any of the children. It was best to know as little as possible. Sometimes I did not even know their names. Later I used to wonder if this one or that one had made it and if their parents had returned.

"Everything you knew that wasn't absolutely necessary was dangerous. In the beginning we were still so naive. No one was prepared for a war, at least we weren't. We had no idea how to run an underground operation when we began. At first there was a rudimentary filing system to keep track of where the children were hiding. We thought we should know where the children were when their parents returned. But then our group was betrayed. I got a signal to go to all my addresses as fast as possible and tell those families that the German police (or the Dutch police for that matter) were coming, that they would have to bring the children somewhere else. Some people did not believe the warning and all their children were deported. At each address I thought to myself, *Am I coming in time, have they already been here, are they waiting for me?* Later I did the rounds one more time and heard that they had come just after I had left. They never did capture the 'blond bitch.' But then I really did have to go into hiding somewhere else in another city.

The people I lived with also wanted me to leave when they noticed I was with the resistance; they were hiding several people who were also in danger. So I went into hiding with your father in Soest. Very close to the German headquarters. And I wanted to get pregnant right away. Then we had to leave that place too because they didn't want to hide people with a crying baby.

"We returned to Utrecht on a little cart pulled by a horse in the middle of the night. Once when we were digging potatoes, I used my bulging belly to my advantage. After the usual harvest a few small potatoes were left behind and we would dig for them. We were caught by the Krauts. 'Come with us,' they told us. I pushed my belly out as far as possible and replied, 'I can't do that.' They let us go home.

"The last months of the war weren't that bad. we were back in Utrecht with Grandmother. We practiced what to do if there was another search, timing it to the second with a watch. Your father and brother had to crawl behind the planks in the attic, the ladder had to be hidden, the hatch shut, and I with my big belly had to sleep on the sofa in front of the hatch. We knew the war was going to end soon.

"You were born at the Rijnlaan. They said I was crazy to get pregnant at that time. They said I would not be able to breastfeed because we had so little food ourselves. They said I was too small and would have a difficult birth. I could not go to the hospital. A Jewish doctor hiding with the neighbors attended the delivery. He had only one eye. I remember exactly how he sat at the foot of my bed with his one eye and said, 'You're doing great, my girl.' I never found out what his name was."

I write down my mother's story as far as I can remember it for my discussion group. I let my mother read it. She immediately writes back on paper torn out of the notebook where she keeps track of the tennis tournament and the progress of the children. In her neat, slanted script unmarred by the usage and spelling errors she hates in my prose, she writes:

"Dear Anja. As I read your piece I have to tell you that I truly appreciate the way you describe the exact circumstances of your birth as written by yourself."

She corrects a few errors I have made, adds a few details, writes that she feels one with me. There are similarities between my work now with oppressed groups and her work back then.

She ends her letter with, "I am writing this in haste, as if I'm being chased. Quickly, before I lose the impulse. I hope it's of use to you. See you soon. Goodbye, my dear. Mother."

5.

One year before she died we made another appointment. We were able to talk again, and the greatest misunderstandings had been resolved.

"I have a birthday present for you," she says and hands me a small square package. "I hope you like it," she adds, more hesitant and unsure than usual. "It's always so difficult to know your taste."

Inside is a watch on a chain. "I thought you might be able to use it when you work or if you're giving a lecture somewhere. Look, you can lay it down in front of you like this," she demonstrates. I nod. "Something is written on the back, I had it engraved." Now I really see how shy she is.

On the backside there are small square letters: "6-1-83. A X A. The wall is down."

I can't speak.

"Do you like it?" she asks.

I nod.

"I did not have the courage to give it to you," she admits. "I've had it in my purse for months now. I thought: *Suppose it isn't true, suppose you don't think that the wall is down.* But it is down, isn't it?"

I nod again and turn around to grab the tea pot.

I still can't bear to have her see me crying.

III.

If only I had known you as a child,
You who are now my child and mother.

1.

It is not easy for her to ask for help. She is proud of being able to stand on her own feet. She is afraid of disappointment and rejection. It has become a part of her life philosophy that people should know *spontaneously* what she needs, otherwise she does not want their help.

So I should have seen that things were not going well, despite her denials. I should not have taken her at her word, *just let me be, don't worry about me,* as she leaned forward in her chair, hands on her stomach. "Why don't you go to the doctor?" I would say over and over again sometimes gently, other times irritably. "Let me be, it will be over in a minute," she would always reply. "Doctors are useless. One says I have an ulcer, the other says I don't. What help is that?" "So go to another doctor," I suggest. "You should keep asking for tests until they can tell you what it is."

"You don't know what you're talking about," she says. "You don't know what it's like, one of those examinations. And there are no results. I refuse to go any more. Give me a glass of milk and it will be over in a minute."

"Warm milk?"

She wrinkles her nose. "Cold."

I should have known that something was wrong when she called off a dinner appointment just before summer vacation.

"I don't feel one hundred percent," she says on the telephone. "What a shame," I answer. "I'll cancel the reservation. Shall I drop by with a bite to eat?"

"No, better just let me be," she says.

"Then we'll see each other when I'm back from Italy," I say.

On my return from Italy I hear her embittered story about the terrible crisis she has suffered.

"What was it exactly?" I ask.

"Pain. Each time in a different place. I could not eat any more. Diarrhea. I must have eaten something bad, or it could have been the heat, which was unbearable."

"Did the doctor come?"

"No," she says, "doctors are useless. And I can't even describe the problem, the pains are so vague."

The cleaning woman calls, saying that she is worried, that my mother never cooks.

"I know that," I reply. "She's told me that she has not cooked since her divorce."

"But it can't go on like this," says the cleaning woman. "Once in a while I used to bring her some stew because she said she liked it. But the third time the pan just stood untouched in the refrigerator for days. Can't you talk with her?"

I try again.

"I eat at the tennis club," she claims.

"What do you eat? Beer?"

"Sandwiches," she says, "and milk. I don't feel like cooking. And usually I'm not even hungry." Her tone implies, *Don't meddle.* If I don't meddle now, she can reproach me later for not paying attention to her when she was sick.

She never asked me for help. The only time I remember is when her old black tomcat was sick, her former cat. She called up in a total panic. "The cat is under the bed," she said, "and he's bleeding from the mouth." She could not reach a doctor. Would I help her call one? "I'm coming over," I said.

I had rarely seen her so upset. I located a veterinarian who held evening hours and went along with her in a taxi, the cat softly moaning in a bag on her lap.

"If he dies, if he dies. . ." she says, "I don't want to

go home alone."

During the treatment, it turns out the cat has an infected tooth, which is pulled while he is sedated. In return we get a limp, warm, heavy black animal that looks dead, his eyes open and his fangs hanging over his lip. "He is so ugly," she says, "but so lovable."

I know how scared she is of being really alone, of dying, or worse, of slowly degenerating. She saw it happen to her own mother, that is to say her father's fourth wife who after his death became senile in a flat she bought when the large house along the Utrechtse Canal proved too much for her. Gradually she lost her mind, the grandmother who had always been so fastidious, so polite and well-mannered, a genteel housewife. Before that she was a publisher and writer of children's books and novels for ladies. At forty-five she gave up her work in order to live with my grandfather, to marry him eventually, and throw herself into housekeeping. Linen napkins and silver napkin rings. Knife rests. Separate dish towels for the glasses and knives. Crystal trivets for the liqueur glasses in Sunday bridge games. A vase of forget-me-nots in the guest room where I used to sleep, a little scared of the stuffed seagull perched on top of the linen closet.

When my grandfather died, she did not want to go on. She lived mechanically because that was the thing to do, but the books she received on her birthdays were never opened, and the meals became makeshift, less carefully planned. Then we noticed she did not cook any more when she was alone. She grew deaf but refused a hearing aid, sitting with a friendly smile when we visited and giving answers that made no sense. My mother placed her in a rest home. She could not take care of herself, had turned off the hot water heater because she never took a shower any more. When they found her sick with pneumonia after an unsuccessful suicide attempt beating herself on the head with a hammer, they had to cut away the clothing that she apparently had not changed for months. "Do you remember what she said when she was lying sick in bed?" my mother asks emotionally. " *Can I give up now?* But then she got better."

Once I went along to visit her in the rest home with other old, senile people. Little remained of the lady she once was. She was ill at ease, avoided contact with the other women, sat like a little bird on a chair in the corner. "There's my mother," she said when she saw my mother. She allowed herself to be fed the soft fruit cookies my mother brought for her. She did not recognize me but sensed she should respond somehow. "Ma'am," she mumbled politely and offered me one of her half-eaten cookies. The gesture reminded me of the Sundays when she bustled about refilling glasses and arranging salty almonds in silver trays. "This is not good for her," my mother said on the way back, "but what else can we do? We can't leave her alone. Last week she resisted a bath by one of the male nurses. She did not want a man to wash her, but they think it's foolish for a seventy-year-old woman to protest. Later that same male nurse came to me and said, *Your mother was a nuisance again this morning, she wouldn't let us dress her.* Then I saw they had put her in a dress that belonged to someone else."

Of course she would protest, she who has always been so neat and so orderly.

"If that ever happens to me, if I ever become like that," my mother says to me, "I'd rather have an injection to put an end to it."

She is scared of death. Scared of going into a slow decline, of losing control, of being at the mercy of others. That is what scares her. She is so scared she would rather bury her head in the sand and pretend nothing was wrong when she first fell ill, until she could not deny it any longer.

She calls me unexpectedly. Usually I am the first to

call, while she waits. "I might as well tell you now," she says. "I just got the results from the hospital tests, and it's almost definitely *not cancer.*"

I suck in my breath. So that was going through her head all this time when she said she did not feel well. She thought she had cancer. "Thank goodness," I say. "Thank goodness, you must be tremendously relieved. But what is the problem then?"

"They don't know yet," she replies.

"And why didn't you tell me you thought you had cancer?"

For a moment she is silent. "Well," she says, "what could you have done if it were cancer? Nothing, right?"

"But wouldn't it have been comforting to have someone to talk to?"

She does not answer. I know what she is thinking: "In the end each of us is alone."

She thinks that having cancer means you will die. If you don't have cancer, you won't die. Now that she seems free from cancer, she expects the doctors to cure her quickly with potions or pills. But the medication makes her queasy, and in addition to her diarrhea she vomits continually. She eats nothing and barely sleeps. The phone rings. The old, familiar notes of reproach are creeping back into her voice.

"I tried to call you five times," she says.

"I went to Bergen with Ernst for the weekend," I say defensively. "From now on I will let you know if I am leaving for a few days, ok?"

"The intestinal infection is getting worse," she says. "My system can't take the medicine. They want to do another test. I don't know if I should agree, those tests are so awful. But they say they can't help me any other way."

"Then you should go," I say. "You can't go on like this."

"You don't know how awful it is," she says. "They wash out your intestines and then they insert one of those tubes...to look inside. It's disgusting. And it hurts."

"Do you want me to go with you?"

It takes her a moment to answer.

"But you can't, with your work," she says.

"I can take time off. My colleagues won't mind filling in for me in a situation like this."

"But do you really want to? No, dear, I can't ask you to do it. A whole day in the hospital and all that mess. It's humiliating what they do to you, inhuman, when you're lying there with your...rear end in the air and the three of them..."

"You're my mother, remember?" I interrupt. "You washed my diapers. And I've had a child too, I've mopped up the poop and the puke. I am not afraid of illness and hospitals, and I don't mind the mess. Wouldn't it be better if someone came along with you?"

"It's very sweet of you to offer," she says, "but no, no, it's better for me to do it alone. I would never impose on someone else."

"If you change your mind, will you call me in the morning?"

"I will," she answers.

And she does. She has had a bad night. If it is not too much trouble, she would like me to pick her up in a taxi and stay with her during the test.

Not since I was very young have I seen my mother naked. Now she steps out of her girdle, her beige underpants with lace, and there she stands, chilled, her arms pulling her sweater around herself. I see her thin white legs with blue veins, the folds of her large belly, with a little pubic hair left. They put her on the toilet in a stall and run a tube through her nose and throat. She retches. They pump a fluid through her intestines. "Jesus, that feels terrible," she says, "as if they are trying to fill me up with air." "Does it smell bad?" she asks when it begins to flush through. "You could go get a cup of coffee until I am finished." "No, it doesn't smell," I say. "I'll stay."

We try to think of things to talk about, but we run out of topics very quickly. My son. Her tennis club. Ernst and I are doing well. "Have you heard anything from your father?" she asks. For years the answer has been no. "Don't you think it's strange, though, that he does not even try to contact his grandson?" I agree as I have done so often in the past. We fall silent. She turns on a radio they've attached to the stall. Classical music. "Yuck," she says. "Sounds like wailing cats." Silence once more.

"I can't stand it any more," she finally says. "Go ask if I have to stay here much longer." Suddenly she regurgitates a stream of fluid. The tube drops out of her nose. "Oh god, oh god," she says.

A nurse comes to mop up the mess. "Doesn't matter," she reassures us. "It happens every once in a while."

My mother leans on me on her way to the examination table.

Two doctors stand ready along with an assistant and a nurse. "Please lie down," one of them says.

"Ok, ok," says my mother. "Not so fast boys, we have time." I am given a chair beside her. She screams when they insert the apparatus into her anus. "Relax, ma'am," says the doctor. "But it hurts!" my mother cries out indignantly. They stop for a moment to give her an injection of Valium. Then the apparatus is inserted again. It is painful. My mother cries and swears and clutches my hand. The doctors concentrate on their work, their foreheads dripping. The apparatus cannot reach the place where her intestines are infected. They withdraw the tube. "Is it over?" asks my mother. "We have to try again with a narrower tube," the doctor replies. "God damn you!" my mother curses. The Valium does not relieve her pain, she is too alert and suspicious to relax. But the drug does make her less inhibited. She begins to cuss at the bastards. *Men.*

"That's enough now," she warns, as if some child is trying her patience, as if she is threatening to slap him in the face. "Just a little more, Mrs. Meulenbelt, we're almost there," says the doctor. "Now we can really see it. Do you want to look too?" "No," answers my mother sharply. They hand me the little scope, and I see the pink folds of her intestines, inside my mother's body.

"A pretty color," I say in an attempt to cheer her up. "Baby pink."

"Pink like a penis," she says, losing all her inhibitions. I am a little embarrassed, the way I used to feel when my mother would tell off-color jokes after too many beers or when she acted up in a restaurant, stuffing napkins into her purse as if she was tired of acting too proper, too ladylike. She pulls the same face as when she bought sausages from the butcher and called out loud, "Which of the gentlemen here is the biggest *penis popularis*?"

"We'll be finished very soon now," says the doctor, unperturbed. The nurse giggles briefly. "Ow, ow," she yells again as they pull the tube out, "God damn it, how can you torment an old woman like this?"

I help her into the taxi. With her fur coat on she has regained some of her dignity, but she is still drugged and sniffles into her handkerchief. She takes my hand and squeezes it.

"I'm glad you came along," she says. "My daughter."

The diagnosis is not favorable. She will go to the hospital and start taking Prednisone, but if that does not help, part of her infected large intestine will have to be removed. "I don't want an operation," she pleads.

At first the treatment seems to work. Her appetite returns. She eats two, three sandwiches at every meal, gains weight, hoards sugar cubes so she can add three to every cup of tea. She begins to talk about food again, plans to start cooking when she returns home, wants to eat out with me in the city again, picks fights with the other women in her hospital room. She has lived alone for such a long time she is not used to taking other people into consideration. When she is lying near the wall she wants the curtain open between her bed and the bed beside her so that she can look outside through the window. But when she gets a bed near the window, she wants the curtain closed for greater privacy. "What a selfish woman," she complains when the new patient next to her wants to have the curtain open to look outside, which is exactly what she wanted when she occupied that place. "She only thinks of herself."

When the quarrels escalate and she is found tugging at the curtain while another patient is pulling it from her hands, she is transferred to a single room. There she complains she has no one to talk to.

She seems to be improving. She is allowed to go home. But after a few weeks the Prednisone is discontinued and she has an immediate relapse. Bleeding, panic attacks in the middle of the night. Her intestines are not healing, they are dying.

She knows she cannot escape an operation. It is the first time for her. She is gloomy, talks about the time she will not be around any more. She talks about falling down a deep hole. She thinks she will never resurface. "It's not as risky as it used to be," I reassure her. "You shouldn't be alarmed by all those stories. I've had general anesthesia twice now, remember? Once for appendicitis, once for my sterilization. It's kind of nice. You just have to let yourself go."

But relaxing is the furthest thing from her mind. She believes in staying alert, paying attention because if you don't watch out they will do all sorts of things behind your back. And then there is the question of money. Her insurance won't cover all the expenses, and she will have to pay extra. "So what?" I ask her. "You have enough money. And you should ask for a telephone and a television, of course."

"That money will belong to you and your brother soon," she says. "I would like you to pay off your mortgage so at least your house will be your own. Then they can't touch you any more, you'll have your freedom."

"I'd rather see you enjoy the money," I respond. "You don't have to worry about me. I can manage just fine with what I earn."

"But still," she says, "if you are ever on your own like me, or if you lose your job, don't you think it's important that you won't have to hold out your hand for money and that no one can tell you what to do? The money is yours, I want you to have it," she says and squeezes my arm. "Life has not been easy for you. And besides, it is the least I can give you since I did everything else all wrong."

Again I bring her to the hospital. This time she is given a room by herself right away.

For a day after the operation she is euphoric. She has no pain. But then she sinks into a depression. "They promised me I would be better," she says, "but I feel as terrible as ever."

"It was a long operation," I say. "You have to give yourself time to recover. You have to get over the narcosis. And your body has to adjust to the fact that part of your intestines is gone. It has to heal, start functioning again." But she remains angry, angry that she is only allowed to drink, angry she is not allowed any strawberry milkshakes, angry that I refuse to sneak in any shakes for her.

"How do they know what's good for me?" she says. "What do they know? Nothing, right?" She looks at me, waiting for my affirmation of her complaint, and when I say nothing she shrugs her shoulders. I recognize that face from long ago: *You're no help.*

At night she barely sleeps, but she refuses sleeping pills. "Then I will fall into that black hole," she says. "Each time I feel as if I will never return."

She prefers to stay awake, taking small cat naps. But her nights are long. She has no concentration for reading. Television bores her. She is moody when I arrive late for my visit, when I skip a day because I have too much work. "So call me," I tell her. "If you want, you can call me in the middle of the night."

"I'm too tired to call," she replies.

I try to think of ways to entertain her, but it isn't easy. I can't bring her sweets, and she won't read. I suggest contacting her friends to visit her, but she refuses. If it does not occur to them to visit, she does not want to see them. She sets the flowers I brought for her behind her back, out of sight. The only thing that temporarily satisfies her is a magazine featuring an interview with me. "You look much nicer than you used to," she says, scrutinizing the photo that accompanies the article. Then she arranges the opened magazine on her bedside table so that the doctors can see it when they stop by.

Fortunately she is allowed to go home. The daily trips to the hospital are becoming more trying for me. When I leave, her moodiness has rubbed off on me. Once she is back home I hope to break her dependency on me gradually. I won't visit every day. And when she has recovered sufficiently to go to the tennis club, we can make do with a visit once a week, once every two weeks. Maybe she can come to dinner at our place sometimes with Ernst and myself when his sons and my son are there. The one time she hauled herself all the way upstairs she was touched by the friendly commotion, the boys running around, Ernst and I both in the kitchen: the kind of family life she had always wanted but never achieved. And now her daughter who seemed to be heading for trouble as an adolescent is sitting at the table with all those boys and actually looks happy. My mother is impressed and maybe a bit jealous.

"I guess nice men do exist after all," she says, looking at Ernst when he can't hear us. "Or does he only seem nice? Is he only pretending to be nice because I am here?"

"No, he's really like that," I say. "Look how much his sons love him," I add as one of them kisses him on his way out, happy to borrow his father's car. "Nice men do exist, but there aren't enough of them to go around."

"You can say that again," she replies.

After several months she has to go the hospital again. Now resigned to the fact, she informs me by telephone. The operation to remove a section of her intestines has not helped; the infection has spread to other areas.

Just last week she said, "They won't ever lure me to that hospital again, I swear over my dead body." But she refuses to eat and still suffers from pain and diarrhea. "I am not going back there," she proclaims to the family doctor who stands there defeated." You'll just have to think of some other cure."

"But Mrs. Meulenbelt," he replies, raising his hands in despair and letting them drop on his knees, "if you react badly to the sulfur medication, and if the Prednisone treatment does not work either, we have no choice but to send you to the hospital."

"How about a diet?" I suggest, knowing how bad her eating habits are.

"Are you eating well?" he asks.

Yes, she nods.

No, I shake my head

."What do you eat?"

"You know, the usual things," she answers vaguely, "a little bite every now and then."

"Instant mashed potatoes with gravy or butter," I say. "Instant desserts. Strawberry milkshakes from McDonalds. Nothing else. No vitamins, and practically no protein. Only fat and sugar and carbohydrates."

She glares at me. I've betrayed her. But when the doctor visits, she is the one who hides the milkshakes I reluctantly bring her underneath the bed.

"Why don't you try toast, grated apples and weak tea for a couple of days?" the doctor suggests. "And then see if your stomach-ache lets up."

"Without sugar?" I ask.

"Without sugar," he affirms.

My mother is furious. "I don't like tea without sugar," she says. "I can't swallow it."

"Well then, a little bit of sugar," the doctor compromises.

I think of the three, four spoonfuls of sugar she shovels into her teacup.

"And I am not going back to the hospital, and I refuse to go through any more examinations," she proclaims as he gets up to leave.

"We shall see, Mrs. Meulenbelt," he replies.

"We shall see, we shall see," she complains bitterly once I have closed the door behind him. "Doctors! What do they know? There must be some cure. Surely there are other kinds of pills."

I go to the kitchen to prepare her something to eat: some grated apple and a few spoons of yogurt with toast crumbled into it.

"Try this," I say. "It might not be as bad as you think." Her hands are trembling, the spoon slips from her fingers. "Come," I say, "I'll help you," and I feed her a spoonful. She opens her mouth and swallows, makes a face. "Sour," she says reproachfully. "If you don't like it swallow it like medicine," I say, feeding her a second spoonful. She opens and closes her mouth but does not swallow, retches, and shakes her head. No more.

"But Dear," I say, still holding the spoon in front of her mouth. "You have to eat *something*." She clenches her teeth together as if she is afraid I will pour it into her mouth if she opens her lips for even a second. Suddenly I break into nervous laughter. "Doesn't this remind you of something?" I ask. "Do you remember how you stood in front of me just like this with a spoon, do you remember saying exactly the same words, 'But Dear, you have to eat *something*?' If you ask me, you look now just as I did back then. Do I need to slap you?"

She cannot bring herself to laugh.

"I never slapped you," she says.

"Sure you did," I say cheerfully, "and more than once. Don't you remember the last time? I was just as tall as you. It was downstairs in the kitchen. You slapped me because I was being rude and without thinking I slapped you back. That was the last time. Don't you remember?"

"That's not true," she insists. "I never slapped you."

I let it go and put the bowl of yogurt down.

"I want a strawberry milkshake," she says.

"I think you have to make a decision," I say. "I will gladly bring you three strawberry milkshakes a day, if that is what you want. But you know it is not good for you, and you'll be more likely to wind up in the hospital."

"I am not going back to the hospital," she says, "but I *do* want a milkshake."

A new problem presents itself. The cleaning woman pulls me aside behind the kitchen door as I am making tea and whispers she has something on her mind. She would like to take a vacation with her husband for one or preferably two weeks, but every time she cautiously brings up the subject my mother acts as if she does not hear. "I can easily arrange a temporary replacement," she whispers, "and to be perfectly honest, I need a break. It isn't easy here, sometimes it makes me nervous. And I don't want to leave when you are all away on vacation, or to wait until September because that's too far away, and we haven't gone on vacation for a whole year. . ."

"I'll see if I can arrange something," I assure her.

"I can hear you," my mother says. "What are you talking about?"

The cleaning woman stands abashed in the bedroom doorway.

"Vacation," I say. "Mrs. Teunissen wants to go on vacation for a week, and I think it's better if she goes when I am still in town. I'm here almost every day and can easily do the shopping for you, and someone else can do the cleaning. Besides, there is not much cleaning to do since you only use the bedroom."

With every attempt at persuasion, she groans. In the meanwhile, Mrs. Teunissen has turned white and clutches the doorpost with shaking hands. She looks as if it is her turn to get sick. My mother, who has seen her, moans even louder and pulls the blankets over her head. Mrs. Teunissen is already hemming and hawing. "If it really isn't convenient..." she starts, but I interrupt. "It's fine. We have time enough to find a replacement, and I can also help out. Everything will be fine."

"Mrs. Meulenbelt," pleads Mrs. Teunissen, "Mrs. Meulenbelt..." But my mother refuses to peep, keeping her head well under the blankets as if she is already dead.

"Well, I guess I'll go finish the kitchen," says Mrs. Teunissen who looks ready to burst into tears any moment.

I nod. She goes.

"Mother," I say, "you can come out now." She says nothing, does not stir.

I pour a cup of tea and wait for her to reappear.

Not long after she becomes so ill that her resistance is worn down. The family doctor has arranged another stay in the hospital. "I can't go on like this," she admits. "At night I can't sleep because of the pain. I have to go to the toilet continually, I can't eat a thing, I'm too weak to climb the stairs. At least in the hospital someone is there to help you at night."

For the third time I prepare to take her there. I also take along her television, pyjamas, puzzle books. "Why don't you pack that, too," she says as I pick up my most recent book from the bedside table. "Will you be reading that?" I ask her. "It seems a bit heavy going for the hospital."

"Oh," she answers vaguely, "who knows, I may get to it." But I know why she wants to take the book along: to show it off, not to read it.

2.

Summer vacation is coming. Ernst and I would like to visit France and Italy, but still have not decided when or whether we should go at all. I am worried. Can I leave while my mother is sick, should I leave? Is it heartless? How sick is she really? Is it temporary or will it be like this for years? What should I expect? I discuss it with the doctors, but they don't know either. It could get better. It could get worse. Right now she is stable.

"We could stay home," Ernst offers. But I really want to go, not only to escape the daily work routine, the mail and the telephone and the housework, but also, to be honest, to be free of my mother just for a while. I had hoped it would be easier now that she is back in the hospital surrounded by a staff who will take care of her. But it's not. Old patterns: the things she appreciated yesterday she takes for granted today. I have to visit daily. When the cleaning woman does not come I have to feed the cat. Once in a while I try to skip a day since her health has stabilized, but when I come to visit the next day she is grumpy, short-tempered, as if I had deserted her for months as in the old days. "Your sister-in-law was here yesterday. Nice of her, don't you think? She didn't have to come, especially since she has three children." I recognize the undertone. I live fifteen minutes from the hospital, my work is only a ten-minute walk from here. I have no family, no small children. "I'll be back again tomorrow, all right?" I assure her. "If it's not too much for you," she says. I try another approach, visiting more often but not for the whole hour. If I come thirty or fifteen minutes before the visiting hour is over, I don't have to glance at my watch all the time which she inevitably notices, and then she doesn't have to say to me, "If you're bored, feel free to leave."

I gave her my book of interviews with various men. She has read a few, some twice even. "You were quite civil to them," she comments, "even though you're such a radical feminist. Do you really trust them?"

"We only picked men we liked," I answer.

"Here," she says, opening the book to one of the interviews, "this Vredeling fellow, you can tell he's not to be trusted, with a mouth like that. Why did you choose him and not Prime Minister Lubbers? At least he has an open face. Or do you have something against Mr. Lubbers? Who is a good politician, in your opinion?"

"I can't say right off the bat," I say. "It doesn't matter what kind of mouth they have, but what party they belong to and what they do. . ."

"So who in your opinion is doing something good?" she persists.

"Listen," I say evasively, "it isn't that simple, I can't just say. . ."

"You are not taking me seriously," she says. "You act as if you can't talk with me about serious things. Don't you talk about politics with Ernst?" I think, and then say cautiously, "I don't like fighting with you."

"Who mentioned fighting?" she lashes out. "I just want a good conversation. You're a coward, that's what I think."

She calls me at work to ask if I can bring her a newspaper and money from the bank to pay her telephone bill. "I wish you had asked me earlier," I say. "I can't leave work before the bank closes. I'm stuck with final exams. Didn't I tell you I would come tomorrow?" "Well, it's only a small favor," she says. "You don't have to come inside, you can just drop the money off downstairs at the porter." "That's not the point," I say. "If I can make it, I want to see you, too, of course, but I have an appointment after work and a meeting with my publisher this evening with three quarters of an hour in between to eat." I can already hear how defensive my voice sounds. "Can't you pay the telephone bill tomorrow? It's not as if you're leaving. Do you have any checks?" She sighs. "I'll try to make it," I say, "but I can't promise."

I borrow the money from a colleague, pick up a hamburger for myself and a strawberry milkshake for her.

"Oh," she says. "I thought you weren't coming."

Sitting straight up in her bed, she collects all her complaints. The door to her room is wide open because she tends to claustrophobia. But I think it also helps her to keep an eye on what's happening outside, to observe that the nurses are taking another tea of coffee break, to determine that other patients are making too much noise. "Shall I close the door?" asks the head nurse, but my mother refuses. "Mrs. Meulenbelt, it is too drafty in here," says the head nurse. "This is a hospital." But my mother does not consider that an argument.

"I pay eighty guilders extra per day," She asserts. "and I will decide whether the window in my own room should be open or closed."

Every time I visit she has a new list of complaints. This morning they brought her custard instead of hot cereal. She hates custard. She had to ring three times before she found someone willing to prepare her some hot cereal. Her medicine arrives exactly forty-five minutes late. This morning the porter forgot about her newspaper. The people next door who can walk stand near the doorway when her television set is on. "I turn it off until they are gone," she says with grim satisfaction. "Why don't you just close your door?" I ask. But no, the door has to be open. With her affected lady's voice she never complains out loud but simply purses her lips.

"You'd think that cooking some hot cereal is just a small favor." I swallow the retort that this is not a hotel but a hospital, and that she is not the only patient when she rings for help and complains that the nurse doesn't come running.

I pack the sixth pair of slippers I've bought for her. She has very clear specifications. Size 8-1/2. "Slippers don't come in half sizes," I tell her, but she insists. No heel, because she can't keep her balance. No elastic, because she can't get them on fast enough. She wants no back on the slipper, no flip-flops, and nothing too wide, either, because she has narrow feet. And definitely no fur lining. "How about the same ones I got for you last time?" I ask hopefully, but those will not do either, because after a week her big toe burst through the seam. "Can you believe how much they charge for those things?" she says. I have tried my best to find what she wants. "Mother dear," I say, holding back my irritation, "it is summer. This is not the season for buying slippers." "Oh well," she says when she sees the new pair of slippers I got her, "I'll just have to make do with these." I let a sigh escape before I can stop myself.

"I know I'm a burden on everyone," she responds bitterly. "My dear, if you only knew how terrible it is to be dependent on everyone." She walks barefoot on her way to the toilet.

In an effort to lighten my load I suggest calling up her old friends, the people from the tennis club, to ask them to visit.

Would she like that? Shall I call? "Ah, no," she says. "The nurses already asked me that, but I told them my daughter visits almost daily. I don't need any other visitors." How about Margreet? You always said you like talking with her." "Margreet talks too much," she says, "and I can't handle that now." She adds conspiratorially, "And not that I have anything against it, but if you ask me she is a lesbian." "What do you mean?" I ask, already on my guard. "Well," she says, "she always puts her hand on my leg and last time even grabbed my hand to kiss it . . ." I look at my mother, her face swollen from hormone treatments and strawberry milkshake dribbling down her chin. "And you know what she told me once, that she hated making love with her husband. . ."

"Mother," I say, "you don't have to be a lesbian to hate your husband. That happens in the best of families."

"All right, I won't say another word, if you take it like that," she says, her mouth pursed up. "I don't mean it that way. I never said anything when you. . .even though it was not easy for me that my daughter. . ."

I stare out the window. If you sit straight up, the tip of a rosebush in the hospital courtyard is just visible. A large yellow rose is in bloom.

"What a gorgeous rose," I comment.

"That's what you said yesterday too," she replies.

The next day my throat is sore. I go through the day, wheezing and coughing. I call my mother. I hear my hoarse voice saying "It's better if I don't come today. If you catch my cough, you'll be even worse off."

"I think we would go on vacation after all," I tell Ernst. "What if we don't travel further than a day's drive and call every day?" "Sounds good to me," he answers. "I'll call some hotels."

I bring her the list with telephone numbers and hotel addresses. I promise to call every day. "We won't go further than a day's drive," I assure her.

She does not look at the paper I give her. "Just put it down over there," she says.

After walking around with a cough for days, I notice that my sore throat disappears as soon as we reach France.

Away from it all, away! Not to have to walk through the hospital hallways, past the porter, left, right, right, left, to room 14 where the door is sometimes open, sometimes closed. I dream about those halls, that door. In Paris we wander around Pere Lachaise. I like churchyards and cemeteries because it is quiet there. We look for the tombstones of Chopin, Proust, Oscar Wilde, Gertrude Stein, and Alice Toklas. At night we dine at the North Terminal. Over plates of shellfish, oysters, and crab I get into a fight with Ernst who claims not to understand why I lose my cool so easily with my mother "Don't you remember how upset you used to get because of your mother?" I ask. But he says he had worked through his relationship with her by the time she fell ill, and there were no unsolved problems when she died. It sounds like a criticism although he doesn't mean it that way. As if I have not tried hard enough. I begin to explain how it feels sitting next to her bed, searching for something to say when she asks: "Tell me something exciting." "So tell her something exciting," Ernst responds. "You always have plenty to say. Talk about your work, or your son, or us." "She does not understand my work," I say. "And she does not understand Armin, either. She can't wait to hear that he's giving me trouble because adolescents are supposed to rebel against their mothers and it would be a great relief if I had the same problems with him that she used to have with me." "So play along with her," Ernst suggests. "Why does it matter to you if she needs to be reassured she wasn't such a terrible mother after all? "I can't stand it," I finally scream out loud, scaring away the boy in the white apron who was about to clear our plates full of empty shells. "That look of triumph in her eyes as if she had found me out when Armin called up one time to ask where I was. That tone of voice, when she says, *So you don't see much of each other, do you? Armin doesn't even know where you are.* All those innuendos when I talk about you and me as if I've finally returned to the right path, as if all those years together with a woman had been a big mistake. The look that says: *I knew it all along.*" "She is jealous," says Ernst, "and isn't that understandable? You've done everything she never dared to do herself." "Exactly," I say. "It's jealousy. She isn't happy unless I am unhappy. When I tell her how well things are going, she won't listen. She is always fishing for trouble."

"But she is also proud of you," Ernst defends her. "She shows your books to everyone, and reads the interviews line by line."

"But that has nothing to do with me, that's to show off that her daughter is a celebrity. She has never had any real interest in *me*. After ten years she still doesn't know what subject I studied although I have told her at least twenty times. A while ago she asked me if I needed glasses yet. I've worn glasses since I was ten years old! She forgot that too. I could strangle her, with all her opinions and prejudices, when she sits there with strawberry dribbling down her chin looking sour no matter how many pairs of slippers I bring her. . ." I start to cough. My throat hurts again.

"Shush, shush," Ernst comforts me, "you still have that cold. . ."

I don't say anything. *Bastard,* I think to myself. *You don't understand, either. You don't know half the effort I make and how much it costs me.* As if he has been reading my mind, he says, "Really, it's not a criticism. If you ask me, you aren't doing such a bad job. She *is* a demanding woman, and it's difficult for you. But you should not let it affect you so much."

The waiter dares to approach our table again. "Would you like some cognac with your coffee?" Ernst asks. I nod.

"You're still angry at her," says Ernst. "But you have opportunities that are not available to her. You can overcome your anger. And once she is gone, you would hate yourself for not doing everything you could. Right?"

"Yes," I say. "That's true."

In the morning I call her from the hotel, before we start driving.

"How is it going with you?" I ask.

"Bad," she says.

"What do you mean, bad?" I ask.

"Just bad," she says impatiently. A silence falls, while I think of something to say. "Where are you right now?" she asks.

"France," I say.

"Yes, I know that," She says, "but where in France?"

"Paris. We're going to start driving soon. Tomorrow I'll call again, if you want me to. Did the doctor say anything?"

"The doctor never says anything," she answers. Silence.

"Did Armin stop by?" I ask.

"No, he's probably too busy with his girlfriend," my mother says.

"Why don't you call him?" I suggest. "If you tell him you'd enjoy a visit, he will be glad to come."

"I'll see," she says. "I'm tired now. I'm going to hang up."

"Talk to you tomorrow," I say, "and Ernst says hello."

"Ok," she says.

Every morning I try to call sometimes from a hotel, other times from a post office where I stand in line with a fistful of change. The conversations are the same. Curt. When I ask her how she is, she does not answer any more. "Stupid question," she says. "What do you want me to say?" "Well," I say, "I'd like to know how you are doing, that's what I'd like to hear." "Why do you want to hear that things are going bad?" she responds.

Occasionally I call the head nurse to hear how things are going. "Not much change," she answers. "The situation is stable." They can't say much but, yes, if there is reason to contact me they will do so immediately.

It takes me at least half an hour to get rid of the chill I feel after one of those conversations. Ernst has learned that I am not good company when I emerge from the telephone booth. He handles me like fragile porcelain until he can see on my face that I'm back with him in France, near the flowering lavender and the fragrant thyme. Haut-Provence. Something is wrong with the exhaust pipe. While it is being repaired we eat in a little roadside restaurant. After waiting for hours to pick up the car, we arrive late at our hotel where it turns out they have misplaced our reservation. The hotel is full. We drive on a primitive road for hours to another place high up in the mountains. I asked the previous hotel to forward any telephone calls or telegrams, because now the number we left in the hospital won't correspond to where we are. When we arrive at the second hotel it is too late to call. I will try in the morning.

Her voice sounds cheerful and high, as if she's been drinking. I barely manage to swallow the question, *How are you doing?* and ask instead, "You sound cheerful, are you doing better?"

"They operated," she says, almost singing, "they operated again, last night."

"Operated where?" I ask in shock.

"Don't know," she says. "Good-bye!" She hangs up.

I call the head nurse. "It was an emergency operation," she says. "An intestinal perforation. No, her life is not in danger any more, but for a while it was critical. We called your son. He was here last night. I think he tried to call you."

I try to reach Armin. When I finally find him, he confirms that he sent a telegram to the hotel. It must have been before we arrived there, but since they forgot to register us they probably did not accept it. "Wouldn't you know it," I say, "the one day we can't be reached, something happens." We discuss the situation. Shall I return home? "I don't think it's necessary," says Armin. "Last night I would have liked to talk with you when they said they were going to operate, but when you did not react to the telegram I decided to go to the hospital, and now things are pretty much back to normal. At least I know where you are. I will call if it's important.

After a day or two, when my mother has recovered sufficiently to answer the telephone, we resume the conversations we had before the operation. Curt. "It still hurts," she says, "and I'm not allowed to eat anything. I sleep badly. When are you coming back?" she asks. "We're driving back on Monday," I answer, "and on Tuesday I'll be with you again. Over the weekend we are going to Aix, to see some friends of Ernst." I hear how I am justifying myself as if I am asking for permission. "I will call you from there." She says nothing. As usual she is the one who ends the conversation.

3.

"Here I am again!" I call out as cheerfully as I can, walking into her hospital room. I lay the flowers on her bed and bend over to kiss her. I see immediately that something is wrong, very wrong. "Is there a problem with your intestines?" I ask. "Yes," she says. "Are you still in pain?" "No," she says and bursts into tears, "but I've been so lonely, you should never have left me alone, I was so lonely, you should not have gone on vacation, for me there will never be another vacation, and you're still young, you can go every year, you could have skipped this once for me. . ." The cleaning woman sitting at her bedside, fills me in: "It was very difficult for your mother, really I tried to come as much as I could, but it was very difficult, without you and your brother also away. . ." She has tears in her eyes too. Two pairs of women's eyes stare at me reproachfully. I feel slightly nauseated, sit down, and say as gently as possible, "But I offered to say home, and then you were mad because you thought I was making a decision you thought unnecessary. Remember?"

It doesn't help. My mother is still whimpering, the cleaning woman passes a handkerchief on to her. "I'll be going now," she says. "You haven't seen your daughter in such a long time, you probably have a lot to talk about." As I stand up she grabs my arm and whispers loudly, so my mother can also hear: "You should never have left your mother alone like that. She was so lonely."

Suddenly rage wins out over the sinking feeling that I've messed up again. How long has it been since I was openly angry at my mother? Years, years. I always swallowed my rage, because the consequences were worse than the momentary relief. The terrible suffering. The oppressive silences. My contortions to make it better again. I preferred to clench my teeth and say nothing until I had nothing more to say.

"Listen here," I say, "I called every day. Why didn't you tell me how bad things were going?"

"Didn't I say things were bad?" she says. "Couldn't you hear it was bad?"

"You always say things are bad," I say, "for months now. Why didn't you say you wanted me to come back?"

"But I didn't know if you would want to," she says.

"God damn it," I explode, "I called every day, I asked if I should stay in Amsterdam, and you said no. I deliberately did not travel more than a day's drive so I could return immediately. You could have gotten Armin to call and ask me to come back, the nurses could have called, you had a whole list of telephone numbers and addresses."

"But I didn't know if you would come if I asked," she says.

"Have I ever let you down when you asked me a favor, when your cat was sick, when you needed shopping done, when you had your examinations, when you had to go to the hospital? Did I ever say no?"

She stares at me suddenly meek as a lamb.

"No," she says, "you never let me down when I asked you."

While I am still standing there, wondering what I have done wrong this time venting my anger on a person who is so ill, she suddenly begins to talk about all kinds of things without any sense of being wronged, without saying even once, "It was only a small favor."

"I'm always happy when you come," she says, "and I'm really grateful that you are here so often and do so much, honestly. . ."

It's my turn to stare at her in amazement.

"Don't you know that?" she says, her eyes filling with tears again. "Nurse, don't I always say how happy I am that my daughter comes to visit so much. . ." The nurse, who has come in to rearrange her I.V., nods. "She often talks about you," she says. "She is really happy that you come, that she can really talk with you, that she has so much support from you."

"My darling," says my mother as she takes my hand, "how is it possible you don't know that?"

These days are almost serene. It was a difficult operation, but everything is going relatively well now. She shows me the plastic bag on her stomach, an artificial outlet for her intestines. "The doctor says that it will be possible to reconnect the pieces of intestine eventually, and then I won't need this thing any more," she says. "And you can even play tennis with it." Her doctor claims this can all turn out for the best. The advantage of the operation is that no large intestine is left that can still be infected. Cautiously we begin to discuss what we should do when she returns from the hospital. Should we try to find help for her at home or would it be better for her to be taken care of somewhere else as she recovers? It is mid-August, light summer weather. I don't have to go to my job yet, I am working on my next book, walk through the city, read the newspapers more thoroughly than usual, sleep late. My brother returns with his wife and children. I call up to warn them that Annie was very angry because we were all away. "I could not get back," my brother says defensively. "The car was registered on my passport, and I would have had to take the children back with me too, and they see their other grandmother so rarely." But my mother has already vented her anger on me and, when everyone is there with her, she sits in bed surrounded by her grandchildren as if it's her birthday, satisfied with so much attention.

No longer dragging my feet as I did before the summer, I walk through the hallways to room 14. The door is usually open, and she sees me coming. Today it is closed. When I enter, for a moment she looks asleep. Then I see that her eyes are open and following me. "Annie," she says to me.

She is slouched sideways into the pillows of her hospital bed. Her eyes are bleary, unable to focus on my face. For weeks now her room has smelled of a mixture of artificial sweetener, the pink-colored drink on her bedside table, and the air of sickness. Shit and sickness. The smell of the diaper pail, long ago.

I sit down next to her, kiss her on the cheek.

"I am Anja," I say. "You are Annie."

She searches my face. "Oh, yes," she says and sinks away again.

I sit down next to her and stroke her swollen, shiny arm. She mumbles something about apples. "An apple?" I ask, "I don't think you're allowed. Shall I ask for some apple juice?" No, she shakes her head impatiently, misunderstood: apples.

Then with difficulty: "Made photos. Want to see." Photos of apples? She nods. "The photographer." She laughs briefly like a girl. "Not allowed," she says. "Asked anyway. Funny, no?" I nod as best I can. She prattles on about a brown bear. Suddenly she talks in her Utrecht accent from long ago. "Little boy," she says to me. Her face turns red, she poops, gurgling, the stench spreads through the room. "Oh dear," she says grinning as if she has done something naughty. This is my mother, my proper, elegant mother who wanted to remain a lady even on the operating table.

Now she doesn't care any more if I am there when the nurse washes her behind, changes the bandages, rubs in the white salve to prevent bedsores. She clasps my hand when it hurts her to be handled by them.

"We're doing what we can," says her doctor. "She really should have another operation, but she is not strong enough in her present condition. There is a fistule and the last piece of intestine, although it's not working any more, is still producing waste. The infection continues to spread."

"But we must not give up hope," he says, although it sounds as if we should. The head nurse from the night shift shakes her head. "I would not count on her recovery," she says. "He's a good doctor," she says, "but he cannot let his patients go, he insists to the very end that there could be a change for the better. We cannot do much, except feed her through the I.V. and made sure she is clean and does not have too much pain."

I discuss with my brother what we should do if there is a plan for another operation after all. Should we agree to this prolonged suffering? What kind of life is left for her if still more has to be cut away? She always said, "If I can't play tennis or drive a car any more, I'd rather end it all." I remember that, but can we judge how much she still values life, the little bit of life that's left in her?

When I stop by again they have brought her to the x-ray room for pictures. "Go on in," says the nurse. "She likes it when you're with her. She has been lying there for several hours. The contrast fluid did not reach her veins, so we had to take new pictures."

It's an awful, hollow room painted a depressing color of green. She is lying on a flat, hard bench and looks like her sick cat in the waiting room at the veterinarian's office. "What's wrong, what's wrong?" she asks, in panic.

"They're taking a photo of your stomach," I say.

"Photo?" she says, "photo?"

I look up at the ceiling she is staring at, all those tubes and gadgets.

"They'll be finished soon," I say, "and then you can go back to your room."

She is restless, shifts her legs, the skinny thighs with too much white skin hanging down. Her hand gropes for something, and starts with surprise when she feels the I.V. in her arm. Suddenly lucid, she looks at me and says, "Poor Anja, how dull this must be for you," and then sinks away, going nowhere, nowhere.

I can tell from her eyes she knows who I am. But the conversations are increasingly confused. Sometimes she laughs aloud about something I don't understand at all, sometimes she is angry, sometimes she is panicky. She is irritated when she wants to say something, wants to have the answer to a question I don't understand.

Sometimes it's better. I help her drink from a glass with a straw. Her hands shake so much she cannot hold anything any more, but today her eyes look clear. She says she is happy I am there. She wants to know: "Who won yesterday?" "You mean at tennis?" I ask. "Was there a contest?" "No, I mean in the hospital."

"How could someone win?" I ask. She knows I don't understand a thing about sports.

"You know what I mean," she says impatiently. "I *know* that some people dropped out. Your brother, did he drop out?"

"He is coming soon," I answer, "to visit you."

"Why?" she asks.

"To make sure you're not alone," I say.

"I'm not alone," she snaps.

Slowly I learn to go along with the babble. It's easiest if I just say whatever comes into my head. Sometimes she nods in satisfaction when I respond with something about parrots or clowns. The drawings made by the grandchildren. "Too many letters on it," she says about one of them. "Some people might object to that." "Fortunately there are more letters," I say. "Otherwise I could not do my work." She nods in agreement; it's a nice thought.

I slowly realize she is dying.

Actually, it was clear from the moment when she didn't care how she looked any more, when she wore a hospital robe, let the first hairs on her chin grow, no longer hid the fact that she wore a small hairpiece bleached blond like plastic. When she no longer tried to control the situation. The moment when she turned inward, no longer paid attention to the outside world. "Why don't you put that down," she said the last time I brought another newspaper interview, without even looking at the picture they had taken of me.

She retreats further and further into herself. Sometimes she is back in her past. "Shoot them," I hear her saying repeatedly. And once she said, "They're coming to get you," as if she wanted to warn me. She is fearful and restless these days. Is it the fear she had always denied during the war? Once she said in Frisian or with a Frisian accent: "Do you want to get into bed with me?"

As she softens, the armor disappears and also her rage. She looks more like the photos that I knew from her youth when she was just a mother or not yet a mother. It is not difficult to sit with her, hold her hand, listen to bits of her past all jumbled together, some of which I recognize and some of which I do not. One time she is mad at her father. "Bastard," she says. I am not sure whether she means my father or hers, or whether they have merged into one person.

The head nurse comes in to ask if the telephone should be disconnected. She does not use it any more. We decide to keep it. She gets restless when her environment changes, when her things are not where she expects them to be. For a long time she wanted to keep her watch on and she is still irritated if there is something on her bed that should not be there.

I sleep a lot now. I am quieter than usual. "You're in mourning," says Ernst. "I know how that feels."

Is that it? The feeling is not painful, not even that heavy. It is not difficult any more to go to the hospital to sit by her bed. Afterwards I sit for hours with a newspaper in a coffee bar at my house, at Ernst's house, without really reading, without remembering anything. It is still August. I see almost no one. I have no desire to talk. My days are filled with mourning.

The I.V. is out. Her veins cannot take it any longer. Now that she is no longer fed intravenously they try to give her solid food. They put it in front of her, ordinary meatballs, a vegetable, a spoonful of mashed potatoes. A dish of pudding. She does not see me when I enter. She has the spoon in her trembling, shaking hand. With the utmost concentration, like a toddler just learning to eat by herself, she aims the spoon at the pudding. "Why don't I help you?" I ask, but she does not see me, does not hear me.

I take the spoon and give her some pudding. She opens her mouth and swallows like a well behaved child. She misses half of it. With a movement I recognize from long ago I scoop the pudding from her chin and put it back in her mouth. After three bites she turns her head away.

The nurse comes in with pills for her to take.

She demonstrates how I can crumble them into the pudding. I hold the spoon up to her mouth again. She swallows, makes a face. She does not like it. With the next spoon, she clenches her lips together. "Come now, Darling," I say, "It's for the pill, to get better." Meekly she opens and closes her mouth without swallowing, and sinks away in a private dream.

"Do you want something to drink, to get rid of the taste?" I ask.

Suddenly she looks at me again, almost lucid, and in her most polite voice says: "Not at the moment, thank you my dear," only to sink back into her own world again.

It is Friday evening. I have already been at the hospital today. Ernst's sons are having dinner with us. We are sitting with our last glass of wine at the table; I am tired but relaxed. The boys have turned on the television. The telephone rings. Ruben, the youngest, picks it up and says, "I will call her," and comes to me: "It's the hospital." While Ernst tells them to turn the television down, I hear the voice at the other end. A crisis. Blood pressure is down. Can I come immediately. My hands turn cold and for a moment everything around me seems to move in slow motion. Micha, the oldest, offers to drive me there with the car. I accept gratefully. We cannot get there fast enough, we have to go through the center of the city with honking cars along every canal and hordes of people out on the town. We keep getting stuck in the traffic. When I walk into the room at first I cannot see my mother among all the people, doctor and nurses crowding around her bed. One of them is trying to jam an I.V. into her broken veins, another is measuring her blood pressure. They can measure it again, it is rising, and the people around her bed relax, begin to talk again, tell me that the crisis is over. My mother is red and perspiring, "I can't go on," she says. "I do not want to go on. I'm going home." My brother arrives with my sister-in-law, and we drink coffee together.

When I leave after about an hour, she smiles angelically at me.

It is early September, rainy weather. The lamp over her bed is on, as if it were a winter afternoon. Sounds of a lawn mower drift in from outside, coffee cups clatter in the hallway. I hear the nurses laughing. The door rattles slightly in the wind. She seems to be listening but hears something other than the things I hear.

The hand without the I.V. gropes for the nurse's bell. She cannot reach it.

"What do you want the nurse to do?" I ask.

I see she is trying to concentrate, but she says nothing.

"Does something hurt?" I ask.

"Yes, it hurts," she whispers.

"What hurts?"

"Two children," she says, "two children."

"What do you want the nurse to do?"

"Get the children."

"But I am already here," I say.

"They must listen," she says, barely audible.

"I am listening," I say.

She is silent.

She does not look up any more when I open the door. I take her hand, but it does not seem to make any difference.

"Do you remember?" she says one time without finishing her sentence.

I sit close by with my head next to hers so I can hear if she says something. Once she opens her eyes. "You have to. . ." she begins to say

"To what?"

"Move away," she says.

I am sitting too close. For a moment I feel as I did in the past: dismissed, unwanted. Then feelings of respect and relief take over. She does not need me any more. It is as if she has departed on a journey to a place where I cannot follow and where she does not want anyone with her.

"Do you know who I am?" I ask one more time, when her eyes are open and searching my face. She does not react. I think it does not matter any more.

"Do you want something to drink?" I ask. Then for the last time she says a few words I can understand loud and clear: "I have nothing to say here."

After that she does not talk any more. Occasionally a corner of her mouth trembles when I say something like, "I'll be back tomorrow," as if she is trying to smile.

She breathes with a rattle. There is mucus in her windpipe. I have seen that taking care of her body is a lengthy ritual with the nurses bathing and rubbing her, attaching new plastic bags to her stomach, siphoning the mucus from her throat. She lies nude under the sheets and lets them take care of her without even a groan.

But her breathing is heavy, every breath separate, irregular. Once as I sit beside her I think she has taken her last breath, because it takes so long for her chest to rise again.

At night I huddle close to Ernst's warm body.

On Tuesday I decide not to go and give myself a day off. But the next morning I am worried when I open the door to room 14. For a moment I think, surprised, that she has curled up into that position by herself like a child with her head buried in the pillow, but it's the nurses who turned her on her side. Her breathing rattles softly, not the tearing sound I heard last time, and she sucks on something imaginary once in a while. She is peaceful. I sit there for a while, pull up the blanket to cover her hand.

"The same," says the nurse. "We suction the mucus from her respiratory passages, we give her liquids and nourishment, try to move her as little as possible. She does not struggle any more when we wash her." After work I stop by one more time. She is lying there, exactly the same. Her cheeks are red and warm.

My sister-in-law and I speak on the telephone. No change. I call my lover. "I'm working late tonight," he says. "I'm going to bed early," I say. "Let's meet tomorrow."

The telephone wakes me up. I know immediately that it must be the hospital. I glance at the clock as I reach for the phone beside my bed. One thirty a.m. "Hello, this is the Prinsengracht Hospital. I am calling about your mother, I am sorry to call so late. . ."

"She is doing worse," I say matter-of-factly."

There is a brief silence on the other end. "Your mother has just died," she says.

I don't know what to say. A jumble of emotions and thoughts. "It is finished," I think in capital letters, as if death evokes in me an archaic language that is not mine. And then a foolish thought: I don't have a coat to wear to the funeral. And: she died alone without me at her side. And: naturally it would happen exactly on the day when the new students arrive. And: I don't have a mother any more. "We couldn't call you earlier," says the nurse. "It just happened a few minutes ago. She took one deep breath and then she was gone. Would you like to come now or in the morning?"

"Tomorrow morning," I say, "if that's all right."

"Yes," she answers, "it will give us a chance to pre-pare her."

I thank her for the call, for her concern. I agree it is better this way and ask: what is it like for the nurses on the floor after caring for her for so many months. "It is sad for us, too," she says, "especially if you saw her recover and then come back to the hospital after a few months. You never get used to it." When I hang up, I notice my hands are shaking and my knees trembling. And there is something unexpected, an overwhelming silence. A thundering absence I do not recognize. She was always there. Always. Even when I hated her and did not see her for months. Even when I tried to detach myself from her, to escape her. She was always alive and breathing somewhere. Even in the last days, curled up inside herself, she breathed, rasping and struggling. Now there is only the swirling in my head. She is not here any more. My mother is dead. The umbilical cord has been cut for the second time, decisively.

I try to call my brother. No answer, their phone must not be ringing loud enough. Ernst does answer. "She died," I say, "just now."

"Oh no," he says. "Was it a shock? It feels strange, doesn't it?"

Yes, I nod over the phone. I can't talk.

"Shall I come over?"

"Yes," I answer in a small voice, "please."

"I'll call a taxi," he says.

I walk to the refrigerator and pull out a bottle of white wine. I try to think about her lying there in the hospital bed, her lifeless body. I can't recall her face. She is gone. The bond is broken.

"Can I walk in as usual?" I ask the nurse. She nods.

"Shall I go with you?" she asks, "or do you want to go alone?"

"Alone," I reply.

She is lying flat on her back, a sheet pulled over her worn-out body up to her chin. A rolled-up handkerchief prevents her mouth from dropping open. All the color has drained from her face; it looks like marble, with a pale yellow glow.

"You can touch her," says Ernst after holding his hand

to her cheek. I stroke the soft gray hair that has grown in place of her hair which used to be permed and dyed. It feels as it did yesterday. But her skin is cold. Cold.

My brother comes, my sister-in-law. One by one, we cry.

Even Ernst who has only seen her a few times. Someone brings us coffee and stays to tell how she died. They take their time for this and do it in a friendly way. But I also know that we have to clear the room as in a hotel, by eleven o'clock.

"Ok, I'll go," I say. "I'll pack her things."

A few books. The newspapers can stay. I open the closet, take out a bag and stuff it with everything that has to go. The silk pyjamas she never wore, her bathrobe. I leave the underwear, the slippers with one toe ripped open. I look for the rings and her watch among the odds and ends in her dresser, between the medicines and hoarded sugar cubes. The whole time she lies there on the bed, with her marble face and says nothing.

"Do you have everything?" I give them the things, walk back for the television, and again for her fur coat, and one more time, empty-handed, to touch her cold cheeks for the last time and her soft hair.

Outside we blink into the September light as if we are coming out of a movie theater. "The striped blouse she is wearing now will be all right for the funeral," I told the nurse.

Ernst makes coffee for us at home while we think what remained to do.

She never talked about her own death despite the allusions she made to the time when she would not be here any more. Is there a will? Did she want to be buried or cremated? My brother calls the lawyer. There was a will, but she retracted it. In her safe we look for papers. I find the bill for my grandmother's burial which was arranged by my mother. I think this is what she wants for herself. Wanted. "Would have wanted," I say. I still have to get used to the tenses. We call the undertaker. Within an hour he is there. Decisions: the coffin, the cemetery, the text for the announcements, the number of envelopes.

"Solid oak," I suggest, "not varnished particle board. She thought my paperbacks were not real books because they weren't properly bound, like her romance novels. And she should have a separate grave at Zorgvlied. I know Zorgvlied, it's an old place, not as bare and geometric as the newer cemeteries, more intimate.

We have little time to reflect on the wording of the announcement and the obituary in the paper. I have them delete "departed from us," and replace it with "deceased." "To our great sorrow" stays. We call up a few people. The cleaning woman sobs that it's awful. A friend from long ago is surprised, didn't even know how sick she was. And now she has died so quickly?

"Would you like to choose the burial plot yourselves?" My brother hesitates, but I say, "Let's do it." I want to choose the place myself and the tombstone. I want her to be carried with us walking behind her, I want us to be there when the coffin is lowered.

"Would you like to choose the music?" That too. Ernst helps, because we can't decide what kind of music it should be. She hated classical music. Ernst looks at the few records she owned. "Is this something?" he asks and plays the record: a melancholy jazzed up version of "On the Windmill of Your Mind," and I also find a swing version of "Are You With Me."

The man who is in charge of selling us a grave points out places and lists the varying costs, types, sizes and regulations for tombstones.

I read the names on the stones, Christian names, Jewish names: Sajet, Levi, Isaacs. The fourth place is across from a colorful stone with a mosaic in blue, yellow, and red. "Some people like that sort of thing," says the man. I hear my mother's voice: "Dear, why don't you wear something cheerful, you're always wearing those somber colors as if life isn't somber enough already."

"This one," I say, "here."